T0113630

Playforms

by
James Saunders
and
Robin Rook

CAMBRIDGE
UNIVERSITY PRESS

CAMBRIDGE UNIVERSITY PRESS
Cambridge, New York, Melbourne, Madrid, Cape Town, Singapore,
São Paulo, Delhi, Dubai, Tokyo

Cambridge University Press
The Edinburgh Building, Cambridge CB2 8RU, UK

Published in the United States of America by Cambridge University Press, New York

www.cambridge.org
Information on this title: www.cambridge.org/9780521588584

First published 1997
7th printing 2008

A catalogue record for this publication is available from the British Library

ISBN 978-0-521-58858-4 Paperback

Transferred to digital printing 2010

Prepared for publication by Paren & Stacey Editorial Consultants
Designed and formatted by The Wadsley Workshop
Cover design by Newton Harris

Performance
For permission to give a public performance of any of the plays in *Playforms* please
write to Permissions Department, Cambridge University Press, The Edinburgh Building,
Shaftesbury Road, Cambridge CB2 2RU.

Contents

Introduction

A play is a way of telling a story to an audience. In telling the story, the play-wright wants to have a certain effect on the audience – to make it laugh, perhaps, feel sad or angry or think about life in a particular way. There are many different ways of telling the same story and a playwright has to choose one: a farce will make the audience laugh, a fantasy might make it sad, a morality play could give it grounds to be angry and a Brechtian form will ask the audience to judge what it sees.

Imagine you are going to write a play about someone who hasn't done a piece of homework. Here are a few possible plots: the student makes up an excuse for not giving in the work and when questioned by the teacher, the story becomes more and more elaborate and grotesque, until . . . Or the student gives a lame excuse and is ridiculed by the teacher, until it comes out that something tragic has happened at home, when . . . Or the class has agreed that it doesn't approve of homework and goes on a homework strike, until the teacher . . . Or, while the students are discussing their homework with the teacher, we can also hear their thoughts, which have nothing to do with homework . . . Or the student has a genuine excuse but the teacher doesn't believe it, until . . .

Before you start writing a play, you will have to ask yourself some questions: 'Do I want people to find it funny or sad or tragic? Do I want them to look for a moral in it? Do I want it to seem real like life, or not quite real like a dream, or so outrageous and ridiculous that the audience knows it could never have happened? Do I want the audience to sympathise with any of the characters or feel angry with them or laugh at them?' Not only will you need to know what your intentions are, but you will also have to ensure that the audience knows too and will therefore react to the play in the way you intend – that it won't laugh at a tragedy or cry at a comedy.

To achieve this understanding, drama has established certain forms and each form uses certain conventions. Of these conventions, the most important is the kind of language to be used. Will the dialogue be in verse or prose? Will it be poetic and use language which is expressive but rather literary? Or will it be naturalistic and use the language of everyday life? Whatever the convention, it will help the audience to know how it should react. Look at the opening lines of some of the plays in this collection and see if you can tell from them what kind of play it is going to be.

The plays in *Playforms* have been written to illustrate some of the possibilities open to a playwright. In general, plays are seldom purely of one form or another; the categories often overlap. Originally, the division between tragedy and comedy was absolute, but gradually it became blurred. In Shakespeare's plays, for instance, it is possible for an audience to laugh at some parts of a tragedy and to cry at a comedy. Some of his plays fit into neither category because a tragic situation can be given a happy ending and a serious note can interrupt a humorous scene. Nowadays, there are as many kinds of play as there are playwrights, just as there are as many characters as there are people. It is, however, useful to be able to make general distinctions.

As the word 'naturalism' suggests, it is intended to be as representative of ordinary life as possible. The dialogue, for instance, will always be in prose and use colloquial language. This may sound easy, but it is not just a question of copying something that has happened. How do you represent on stage in fifteen minutes an incident which took place at sea in real life and lasted fifteen hours? The purpose of a morality play is clearly to ask an audience to think about right and wrong, but although the purpose is serious, the means of doing it might well be funny. Although an absurd play may seem to be ridiculous – one such play had the main character buried up to her waist and then up to her neck in sand – it can make an audience think. A melodrama exaggerates life and, like life, can be both funny and sad; whereas a farce's sole purpose is to make people laugh. A Brechtian play makes it clear that the audience is watching a play and should be critical of what it sees, rather like a parable or fable. A fantasy is unreal and must appeal to the audience's imagination, like a fairy tale. These are a representative selection of the many forms to be found in modern drama. You will find an example of each of these in *Playforms*.

James Saunders
Robin Rook

January 1997

Dog Accident

Naturalism

A naturalistic play is one that is written as if the story had happened in real life. In staging it, the actors will try to seem just like people one might meet outside the theatre. The extreme case of a naturalistic play would be one that would be mistaken for real life if it were performed in a real life setting.

In the theatre, even the most naturalistic play has to follow certain conventions. It has a dramatic 'shape' which real life doesn't have: for instance, a play has a beginning, a middle and an end whereas real life goes on and on; in a play, only the incident shown can be seen whereas in life things are happening simultaneously all over the world. A play therefore has to condense time and exaggerate effects; anything which is not relevant to the action is left out. The conventions are hidden but they are still there. Can you see them in *Dog Accident*?

No playwright wants simply to present a slice of life. The writer wants the play to do something to the audience, to involve its emotions or make it think in a particular way. What do you think were the playwright's intentions in writing *Dog Accident*? It shows how four young people might react to a commonplace situation, but it gives only one possibility. If you improvise the scene and react to it in your own way, it will be interesting to see how the course of events differs.

A version of *Dog Accident* was in fact performed some years ago in the street of a shopping area in Liverpool. The 'dog' was radio-controlled to whine and twitch. A small crowd gathered, mostly at a distance, not wanting to risk getting involved in what was happening. Then some people came closer: one bystander entered into the dialogue, another covered the dog with a blanket before walking away. Someone called the police. When they arrived, the policemen were at first stern. ('What's going on here?') When told it was only a play, they became jolly. It was as if they had decided to act a different kind of policeman and, being in uniform, they knew that the audience – their audience now – was waiting to see how well they played their parts. Afterwards, the actors, the director and the author discussed whether they had cheated in pretending that the play was real. They decided that perhaps they had. Were they right? What do you think?

1

Dog Accident
by
James Saunders

CHARACTERS
JOHN
ALEX
PETE
MATT

SETTING
A city street.

TIME
Late afternoon.

(A street. Traffic. A sudden screech of brakes, the yelp of a dog.)

JOHN   Look out!

ALEX   Oh, no!

PETE   What was that?

MATT   Look. Over there.

(They walk across to where a dog lies in the gutter.)

ALEX   Poor little tyke.

PETE   What happened?

MATT   What do you think happened?

PETE   Run over was it?

JOHN   Brilliant. No, it dropped dead of a heart attack.

PETE   I didn't see it . . . Looks dead, doesn't it?

(PETE gingerly touches the dog with his foot.)

ALEX   Don't do that! What are you doing?

PETE   What?

ALEX   Don't kick it.

PETE   I wasn't kicking it, I was just sort of nudging it. To see if it's alive.

ALEX   Well, don't. Leave it alone.

(Pause)

MATT   That car should've stopped. Did anyone get the number?

JOHN   What good would that do?

MATT   It should've stopped. We could report it.

JOHN   It was a K reg. MTP something. White Fiesta.

MATT   Fiesta? It was a BMW!

JOHN   It was a Ford.

MATT   It was a BMW. You can't mistake a Ford for a BMW. Different style altogether, different trim, what are you talking about?

JOHN   I only got a glimpse.

MATT   Then why say it's a Ford?

JOHN   It looked like a Ford to me! I only saw it from the back.

MATT   They're totally different from the back.

JOHN   All right! Forget it!

(PETE is crouched by the dog.)

PETE   Do you think it's dead?

JOHN   I thought you did a First Aid course.

PETE   I did.

JOHN   And you can't even tell if a dog's dead? Go on, give it some mouth-to-mouth.

PETE   Very funny.

ALEX   Leave it alone.

PETE   It's still warm.

JOHN   Brilliant.

ALEX   Just leave it alone. Stop mauling it about.

PETE   What's the difference if it's dead?

ALEX   It's not dead.

PETE   How do you know?

ALEX   How do you know it is?

PETE   Well, it looks dead to me.

MATT   Are we going, then? We'll miss the start of the film.

PETE   So are you going to report it?

MATT   What for?

PETE   I thought you said you were going to.

MATT   I said someone could. I didn't say I was going to. Anyway, we didn't get the number.

JOHN   I told you, MTP with a K reg.

MATT   And you thought it was a Fiesta. And it wasn't white, it was off-white.

JOHN   It was dirty.

MATT   It was off-white!

JOHN   I was only looking at its plate.

MATT   Are we going, then?

PETE   Didn't someone ought to report it, though?

JOHN   Who to?

PETE   I don't know. Police? RSPCC?

JOHN   RSPCC!

PETE   I mean A. We might get a Crimewatch award.

JOHN   For telling them a dog's been run over? Don't be daft.

PETE   Well, it's a crime.

JOHN   Running a dog over?

PETE   Not stopping, the car not stopping. That's a crime. Isn't it, Matt?

MATT   No. It's an offence.

PETE   Same thing.

MATT   It's not the same thing. If it was the same thing they'd call it the same thing, they wouldn't have two different words for it, would they?

PETE   I don't know.

JOHN   Anyway, it's only a mongrel.

ALEX   What difference does that make?

JOHN   I mean, it's not valuable, it's not as if it's a pedigree dog. Pedigree dogs can cost a lot of money. This is just a dead mongrel. Big deal.

ALEX   It's not dead.

JOHN   How do you know?

ALEX   It moved.

PETE   I didn't see it.

ALEX   You weren't looking. It moved its leg.

PETE   Are you sure?

ALEX   Of course I'm sure.

PETE   Let's have a look . . . It's not doing it now.

ALEX   There! D'you see that?

PETE   You're right . . . So it's not dead.

JOHN   Brilliant diagnosis. Give him the Nobel prize for Medicine.

(Pause)

MATT   Rigor mortis.

JOHN   What?

MATT   Rigor mortis, that is. It's dead all right. Come on.

PETE   But it moved its leg. Look, there it is again.

MATT   I'm telling you, it's rigor mortis. Like when a chicken has its head cut off. It keeps on running about.

PETE   With its head off?

MATT   Course it does, it's a well-known fact.

PETE   I've never heard that.

MATT   Well, it's true.

PETE   I don't see how it can do that. It hasn't got a brain, has it? Not with its head off.

JOHN   You haven't got one with your head *on*.

PETE   Very funny.

MATT   It doesn't need a brain. It runs about on its nerves. That's what's happening there. So are we going or not? Are we staying here all night?

JOHN   OK, let's go . . .

(JOHN **and** MATT **start to go.**)

You coming, you two?

PETE   We'd better go. You coming, Alex?

ALEX   Not yet.

PETE   Why not? . . . When, then?

MATT   What are you doing, you two? Are you coming or not?

PETE   Alex wants to stay a bit.

JOHN   What for?

ALEX   Till it's dead.

MATT   It is. I told you. It's as dead as it can get. How much deader do you want?

PETE   Come on, Alex. We'll miss the film.

ALEX   It's not dead.

PETE   What makes you think that?

(PETE **moves closer to the dog.**)

ALEX   Leave it alone! Don't touch it!

PETE   He says it's not.

JOHN   What?

PETE   Dead.

JOHN   Oh, God . . .

MATT   If you lot aren't coming, I'm going.

JOHN   Come on! What's the matter with you?

PETE   Come on, Alex.

ALEX   There goes its leg again.

PETE   Is that true? Honest? About chickens?

MATT   It's a scientific fact.

PETE	Does it work with anything? I mean, what about a giraffe? That would look funny, wouldn't it?
MATT	Are we going or not?
JOHN	Yes, let's go. Nothing more to see.
PETE	You coming, Alex?
ALEX	No. Not till it's dead.
PETE	What difference does it make?
ALEX	I don't know. Someone ought to stay with it, that's all.
PETE	Why? There's nothing you can do, is there?
MATT	It was the dog's fault anyway.
ALEX	What difference does that make?
PETE	I don't see that, Matt.
MATT	Don't see what?
PETE	How you can say it was the dog's fault? You can't blame a dog.
MATT	It ran into the road, didn't it?
PETE	I know it did, but . . .
MATT	Well, then. If you run into the road you're likely to get run over, aren't you?
PETE	Yes, but the dog needn't have known that. What I mean is . . .
MATT	It shouldn't have been out anyway, without a lead. That's an offence.
PETE	But you can't blame the dog for that.
MATT	Why not?
PETE	Because it's a dog! You can blame the owner; you can't blame the dog!
MATT	I'm not blaming the dog. I'm saying it was the dog's fault.
JOHN	I'm not hanging about here any longer. I'm not missing the start of the film for a dead mongrel. You know what you are, Alex?
ALEX	What?
JOHN	You're one of those ghouls. One of those people who hang around accidents. You're a ghoul.

ALEX   Did you hear that?

JOHN   What?

ALEX   It made a noise. A sort of whine.

PETE   It did, you know. I don't think you can call that rigor mortis.

JOHN   Come on, Matt. Let's go.

(JOHN and MATT move off a little, but stop to see if the other two will come.)

ALEX   It's not that I'm a ghoul. It's just that . . . someone ought to stay with it, that's all!

MATT   He's just the same in Biology. And you remember that one-eyed kitten we found in the playground, and he insisted on taking it home.

JOHN   And his dad drowned it.

PETE   Look, it's shaking. Look at that. Why's it doing that?

ALEX   It's dying.

JOHN   I tell you what, Alex: you've got yourself a career, I reckon. You can go round the country looking for dying animals so you can stay with them. There's a job for a lifetime there, maybe the Council will take you on.

MATT   Come on.

JOHN   Here, Alex!

(JOHN puts his foot on something.)

There's a dead ant here! You can take care of it when you've finished with the dog! We'll see you later!

(MATT and JOHN go.)

PETE   They're off.

(ALEX nods.)

Do you think it'll be long?

(ALEX doesn't answer.)

PETE   Look at its leg going.

(PETE is getting bored. He wants to leave. He looks round, walks off a step or two and waits. He starts to whistle, then stops.)

You've got to keep a sense of proportion. That's what my dad says. All the things happening all the time, you can't take them all in. I mean, you'd never stop feeling sorry for things, would you? People. You've got to draw the line, my dad says. He gives something to Oxfam once a year and that's it. That's his limit. He says life's too short.

(Pause. ALEX crouches down to the dog and puts a hand on it.)

Is it breathing?

(ALEX doesn't answer. PETE goes back to stand over the dog, looking down at it. Pause.)

Did you hear that? . . .

(Pause)

It's stopped shaking.

(ALEX stands up.)

ALEX   It's what they call 'bearing witness'.

PETE   What is? . . . Do they?

(Pause. Then ALEX moves suddenly away.)

ALEX   Come on, then! We'll miss the start of the film.

PETE   Is it dead?

ALEX   'Course it's dead. Stupid animal. Could have caused an accident. Come on!

(ALEX goes. PETE gives one more glance at the dog, and follows him.)

The end

Whose Friend are You?

Morality

The play presents the Seven Deadly Sins, which are Envy, Sloth, Avarice, Wrath, Gluttony, Lust and Pride, and Everyman. Everyman has been split into a contemporary man and wife. The Sins appear in their true colours at the end. Can you identify them?

Although the characters are personifications, each representing a different sin, they have been given human characteristics and should be presented like ordinary people with one dominant, distinguishing feature. They should be acted with zest and a sense of fun. The New Year's Eve party scene provides an opportunity to include improvisation and since the resolutions are in verse, they could be set to music and sung. (The words of one set of characters, for instance, follow the tune of *Good King Wenceslas*. Can you identify it?)

Clearly the suggested staging is not naturalistic but is based on a convention of the Middle Ages, when morality plays were very popular. There are 'mansions' representing different locations, which share a common acting area. For the sake of simplicity, chairs are used to represent the different characters' homes and there is no reason why placards should not be hung above them saying, for instance: 'Ego's Home'. The space in front of them is not specific and can be used for any situation.

The moral or serious element is kept well beneath the surface and only really emerges in the *Epilogue*. The play's sting is in its tail. What is it?

Whose Friend are You?
by
Robin Rook

CHARACTERS

House No. 1   MR EGO
     No. 2   MRS WITHIT
             MR GRUBBER
     No. 3   MR YOUNG
             MRS YOUNG
     No. 4   MR FATSO
             MRS SLOB
     No. 5   MR BASHER
             MISS BIMBO

SETTING
Anywhere.

Nine chairs, arranged in a semi-circle, represent five houses. Only those for No. 3 face the audience.

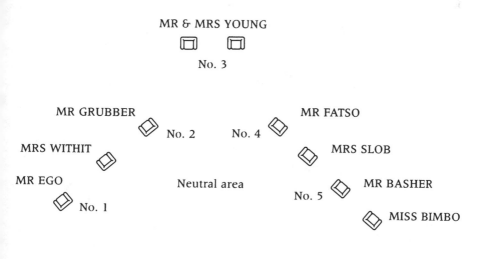

MR & MRS YOUNG

No. 3

MR GRUBBER   MR FATSO

No. 2   No. 4

MRS WITHIT   MRS SLOB

MR EGO   Neutral area   MR BASHER

No. 1   No. 5   MISS BIMBO

TIME
New Year's Eve.

(**The characters remain in their chairs throughout unless they are involved in the action which takes place in the neutral area and is mimed where necessary.**)

MR Y   (**Rising**) Time to do our duty.

MRS Y   Already?

MR Y   Neighbourhood watch, residents' parking, getting involved . . .

MRS Y   (**Rising**) Socialising.

MR Y   That's what it's all about.

MRS Y   Right.

MR Y   (**Coming forward.**) Where do we start?

MRS Y   (**Joining him.**) Is there a pecking order?

MR Y   We're here to find out.

MRS Y   I always start at the top.

MR Y   Of course, of course . . .

MRS Y   That's why I married you.

MR Y   Naturally.

(**A quick kiss on the cheek.**)

MRS Y   So which is the top?

MR Y   Now let's see . . .

(**They chant like children.**)

MRS Y   Number one is Mr Ego . . .

MR Y   Number two the Withit-Grubbers . . .

MRS Y   Number three is our chez nous . . .

MR Y   Calling for another kiss.

(**A quick kiss.**)

MRS Y   Number four the Fatso-Slobs . . .

MR Y   Leaving only number five.

MRS Y   There, oh dear, is Mr Basher . . .

MR Y   And his sexy paramour!

(**Reverting to normal speech.**)

MRS Y   Not too sexy, I hope.

MR Y   With a name like Bimbo?

MRS Y   At least she doesn't live next door.

MR Y   No, one away.

MRS Y   We'll leave them till last.

MR Y   And start with number one?

MRS Y   But we are number one, darling.

MR Y   The one and only number one!

(A quick kiss.)

MRS Y   It's just the beastly Post Office calls us number three.

MR Y   One should be able to buy an address like a car number.

MRS Y   I'm sure one can if it comes on the market.

MR Y   True, darling, true.

MRS Y   Let's split the difference.

MR Y   Number two.

MRS Y   The Withit-Grubbers.

MR Y   I'll ring.

(He does so.)

WITHIT   Who's that?

GRUBBER   Most like, someone collecting for charity or trying to sell some
thing we don't want. Don't answer.

WITHIT   What if someone else gets in first?

GRUBBER   **(Ignoring her.)** One's as bad as t'other – emotional blackmail –
what better time than New Year's Eve? They'll not get a mite
from me.

WITHIT   **(Kneeling on her chair to look out of the window.)** We
might be missing out.

GRUBBER   Whoever it is, it'll cost you, you can count on that. Pretend
we've gone to bed.

WITHIT   It might be an invitation . . .

GRUBBER   To spend!

WITHIT	There must be a lot of parties tonight . . .
GRUBBER	To which you're expected to bring a bottle – as a guest! I ask you. And if you're fool enough to take spirits you can bet your life the host will spirit it away once your back's turned!
WITHIT	You should know.

(He laughs.)

MRS Y	Ring again. They're still up, I saw the curtains move.
MR Y	I'll give one long blast this time.
MRS Y	Do that.

(He rings.)

GRUBBER	**(Jumping up.)** What the hell! That bell's electric, it doesn't pay for itself.
WITHIT	**(Standing)** That's it. I'm going to answer. Must be important.
GRUBBER	**(Sitting)** It'll cost you.

(WITHIT **opens the door.**)

WITHIT	Oh, it's you. How nice. We had the telly on, didn't hear first time you rang.
MRS Y	**(Smiling)** How do you know we rang twice then?
WITHIT	**(Smiling)** No one would ring that loud first time.
MR Y	We called to ask if you and Mr Grubber would care to join us to see the New Year in.
WITHIT	We'd love to. Your house must be looking so nice after all you've spent on it.
MRS Y	**(Smiling)** How do you know what we've spent?
WITHIT	**(Laughing)** I keep my eyes and ears open.
MRS Y	I'm sure you do.
MR Y	See you before midnight then.
WITHIT	Lovely.
GRUBBER	**(Calling)** Close the door! You're letting the heat out.

(WITHIT **retreats into the house.**)

WITHIT	They're so young to spend all that money. Makes you sick!

GRUBBER   Once spent, gone for ever. Think of that.

WITHIT   **(Sitting)** You make me sick too!

Mr Y   Now for number . . .

MRS Y   Don't say it.

MR Y   Agreed?

MRS Y   Of course.

          (He rings Mr Ego's bell. EGO rises swiftly and comes straight to the door.)

EGO   Yes, what do you want?

MR Y   We wondered if you'd care to see the New Year . . .

EGO   I might, if I knew who you were.

MR Y   The Youngs . . .

MRS Y   Your new neighbours.

EGO   Never heard of you.

MR Y   We live at number three.

EGO   Do you? I hadn't noticed.

MRS Y   Would you like . . . ?

EGO   I'll come – alone, of course.

MR Y   See you, then.

          (EGO shuts the door and returns to his seat.)

MR Y   Not the world's greatest talker.

MRS Y   No.

MR Y   Probably enjoys talking to himself, though . . .

MRS Y   Likes listening to his own voice when there's no one to contradict him. I've met his type before.

MR Y   Now for the Fatso-Slobs.

MRS Y   Do we have to?

MR Y   Can't very well not.

MRS Y   They're so unappetising.

MR Y   He'll drink us out of house and home.

MRS Y	And she'll just sit and sit and sit.
MR Y	But it is New Year's Eve.
MRS Y	And they do live next door.
MR Y	No way out.
MRS Y	Afraid not. Besides . . .
MR Y	What?
MRS Y	They've seen us.

(FATSO **opens the door.**)

FATSO   I say, jolly nice to see you. Come in. Time for a night-cap, what? **(Calling)** Mrs Slob, we've got company.

MR Y   We came to invite you to join us for the New Year . . .

FATSO   Great idea. It's so difficult to keep the wife up after midnight. She don't get peckish like me. Or should I say hen-pecked? **(He laughs.)**

SLOB   **(Joining him.)** That's enough, Fatso. Your laughter exhausts me.

(**To the** YOUNGS.) It's bad enough keeping him stoked up without him letting off.

FATSO   Want a demonstration?

SLOB   Don't you dare!

FATSO   See what I mean?

MRS Y   We're having a little party . . .

SLOB   Tonight?

MR Y   As ever is.

SLOB   At your place?

MRS Y   Yes.

SLOB   Oh dear.

FATSO   It's only next door.

SLOB   **(Yawning)** So late . . . so far . . .

FATSO   I can get the car out – have you there in a jiffy.

SLOB   I'd have to struggle into a dress.

MRS Y   It's quite informal.

SLOB   All right as I am?

FATSO   A housecoat isn't exactly . . .

SLOB   I wasn't asking you.

FATSO   Sorry, old gel, just trying to keep on side.

MRS Y   It's all right by us but I can't imagine Mrs Withit . . .

SLOB   Her? You've asked her?

MRS Y   She is our neighbour . . .

MR Y   And we are new here . . .

SLOB   **(Tearfully)** Why does everyone try to make me do things? Why can't you leave me in peace? Why do you all get at me?

MR Y   I'm sorry if . . .

MRS Y   We only asked . . .

SLOB   I wish I'd never got up!

(She returns to her seat.)

FATSO   **(Confidentially)** She tires herself out, poor dear, very emotional.

MR Y   Try to persuade her.

FATSO   I'll do my best but if I fail, all right if I slip round?

MRS Y   You're welcome.

FATSO   If you'll excuse me now, I must keep her company. Nearly time for another snack!

(He returns to his seat.)

MR Y   That's one less.

MRS Y   I wouldn't count on it.

MR Y   Wouldn't you?

MRS Y   If she can summon up the energy, she'll come. Just imagine, stacks of food for old Fatso and she won't have to lift a finger. Tempting, surely.

MR Y   Perhaps.

MRS Y   You'll see.

MR Y   Now for number five, last but not least.

(BASHER **has heard them and come to the door.**)

BASHER   Who the hell do you think you are?

MR Y   We're the new people at number three . . .

BASHER   I don't give a damn who you are.

MRS Y   You did ask.

BASHER   Don't bandy words with me, young lady.

MR Y   We're not trespassing.

BASHER   You most certainly are! The moment you set foot on my land...

MR Y   There's no notice on the gate.

BASHER   What do you expect? The people I want to keep out can't read.

MR Y   We can both do that, I assure you.

(BIMBO **poses at the door in her negligée.**)

BIMBO   And I bet that's not all you can do.

MR Y   **(Smiling)** Not the sum total, no.

BIMBO   If you'd care to call when Basher's out . . .

MRS Y   We'd love to.

BIMBO   I was using 'you' in the singular.

MRS Y   I see.

BIMBO   I don't much care for the company of my own sex.

BASHER   Sex? Did someone say sex?

BIMBO   Don't be a bore, Basher.

MR Y   If we've called at the wrong time . . .

BIMBO   Why did you call?

BASHER   Yes, why?

MRS Y   We're holding a little party at our place for the New Year. If you'd care to join in . . .

BIMBO   I always join in.

MRS Y   I bet you do.

BIMBO	Fancy dress?
MR Y	Come as you are.
BIMBO	As I am? Just as I am? Really? You mean that?
MR Y	(Smiling) No point in gilding the lily.
BIMBO	I spend half my life under a sun lamp.
MRS Y	And where do you spend the other half?
BASHER	What about me? Am I invited? Because I can tell you now, if I'm not, I'll come all the same.
BIMBO	So subtle, dear Basher.
MRS Y	You're both invited.
BASHER	Hear that, Bimbo? They want me too.
BIMBO	Makes a change.
BASHER	Come on then, get cracking. Best bib and tucker.
BIMBO	See you.
	(They return to their seats.)
MR Y	'Bye.
MRS Y	What a pair!
MR Y	Interesting, don't you think? Just imagine them with the others!
MRS Y	Plenty of choice for everyone.
MR Y	A rich mix, no?
MRS Y	I wonder how they'll get on.
MR Y	They're all neighbours.
MRS Y	And have been for years and years.
	(They sit in their chairs.)
MR Y	We're going to like it here.
MRS Y	Friends make all the difference.
MR Y	They have so much to offer.
MRS Y	Mr Ego is one of us.
MR Y	A proper sense of his own importance.

MRS Y   The Withit-Grubbers make a team.

MR Y   Ambition . . .

MRS Y   And thrift.

MR Y   The Fatso-Slobs know how to enjoy themselves.

MRS Y   They'd be good value on holiday.

MR Y   Indulge yourself . . .

MRS Y   Then sleep it off.

MR Y   Even Basher has his points.

MRS Y   So has Bimbo.

MR Y   (**Smiling**) I had noticed.

MRS Y   Aren't we lucky . . .

MR Y   Having such nice friends.

The New Year's Eve Party

(**The dialogue is improvised since it forms part of a general hubbub. The guests arrive together, the YOUNGS circulate among them. Background music. Typical activities might be:**

EGO: **Keeps to himself, looking disdainfully round him.**

WITHIT-GRUBBERS: **She pries into every corner inspecting the furnishings, he puts a price on them.**

FATSO-SLOBS: **He stuffs himself, she collapses in a chair.**

BASHER-BIMBOS: **He tries to pick a quarrel, she makes passes at the men.**

From a quiet beginning, the party gains momentum until midnight chimes. Silence. On the last stroke, MR YOUNG wishes everyone a Happy New Year. The guests respond, form a circle and sing a verse of Auld Lang Syne.**)

The Resolutions

> **(These could be set to music and sung.)**

MR Y   Now for our resolutions.

MRS Y   Who's going first?

EGO   I am.

MR Y   Great.

EGO   **(Intoning)** I'm going to set myself so far apart
From other members of the human race,
They'll have to make exception when they start
Explaining how it was Man fell from Grace.

> **(Slight pause.)**

MRS Y   Is that all?

EGO   That's all.

BIMBO   Isn't he blissful?

MR Y   Follow that!

WITHIT   No problem.

MR Y   Ladies and gentlemen, the Withit-Grubbers!

> **(They run forward, curtsey and bow like a circus act. The others applaud.)**

WITHIT   Watch my little party trick!
See this piece of Dresden china?
(Aside) It's so lovely, makes you sick!
I'll produce a piece much finer,
It will make the Youngs go green,
Make them feel that theirs is trash.
Watch me now, just watch it lean,
Further, further – oh, dear – crash!
Sorry, dears, it didn't work.
Take it as a New Year token –
(Aside) Envy makes me go berserk –
Promises are made to be broken.

GRUBBER   Watch my little party trick!
First of all, I need ten quid –
Just a tenner, come on, quick!

(**To** BASHER.) Thank you, sir. What am I bid?
Don't hold back, it's all for fun.
Thirteen – fifteen – eighteen – twenty –
Give me thirty and you've won!
(**To** BIMBO.) Thank you, madam, that is plenty.
Here's the prize for you to squander,
Take it as a New Year token –
(**Aside**) Avarice makes the heart grow fonder –
Promises are made to be broken.
(**He returns ten pounds to** BASHER **and pockets twenty.
Applause.**)

FATSO   You've whetted my appetite, Mr Grubber.

MR Y   Come on, Mrs Slob, we're waiting for you.

SLOB   (**Rising**) I'm so tired.

FATSO   (**Stepping forward.**) My resolution is to show how the
irresistible force can overcome the immovable object.

SLOB   (**Joining him.**) And mine to show how the immovable object
never stirs.

(**She lies down.**)

FATSO   Bring me booze and bring me grub.

SLOB   Never stir a muscle.

FATSO   Stuff my belly like a tub.

SLOB   Nothing's worth the hassle.

FATSO   (**Kneeling**) Listen, Slob, I'm fading fast.

SLOB   Try some other wangle.

FATSO   Can't you hear my innards vast . . .

SLOB   Churning like a mangle?

FATSO   If you won't my hunger slate . . .

SLOB   What will happen, Fatso?

FATSO   I'll soon cease to be your mate.

SLOB   (**Sitting up.**) Goodness me, is that so?

FATSO   Hold my hand and wish me well,

SLOB   Now that you are going.

FATSO   One last kiss for me, old gel.

SLOB   One is worth bestowing.

(She holds his hands, he pulls her up. They kiss and lean apart, foot to foot at arm's length.)

FATSO   Got you now, you lazy slut!

SLOB   Am I now your debtor?

FATSO   Gluttony must stuff his gut –

SLOB   Sloth can go one better!

(Stepping back, she lets go of his hands: off balance, he falls backwards. Laughter and applause.)

BASHER   Well done, Slob!

BIMBO   Poor old Fatso!

MR Y   It's your turn now.

MRS Y   You're the last to go.

(BASHER and BIMBO take centre stage like two opera singers.)

BASHER   Don't dismiss me as a mercenary
When, in fact, I'm just an ordinary
Chap, marauding where there's any aggro,
With my hidden cache of arms and ammo,
Terrorising in the name of freedom –
Any cause will serve my ire to feed on!

BIMBO   To a dedicated missionary
I'll appear an extraordinary
Siren, luring hardened politicians,
Television preachers and physicians,
To drop anchor in my den of vices –
Nothing's safe so long as lust entices!

BASHER &   Not a day will pass without some story
BIMBO   Breaking, pornographically gory!

(Silence)

MR Y   **(Taking the floor.)** We will try to emulate
Your good example, friends.

MRS Y   **(Joining him.)** We will keep you up to date
With all the latest trends.

MR Y   Thanks a lot for coming here,

MRS Y   And see you all again next year.

(The neighbours disperse to their chairs. The YOUNGS **come forward and address the audience.)**

EPILOGUE

MR Y   We have nailed our colours to the mast.
Can you say the same?

MRS Y   Is there not some secret from your past
Makes you blush with shame?

MR Y   Have you always to yourself been true?

MRS Y   Never put the blame
Onto someone else?

MR & MRS Y   **(Pointing at the audience.)**

Stand up and be counted.
Whose friend are you?
Are you one of us or one of them?
Give yourself a name!

The end

Alas poor Fred

Absurd

Most plays, even when their form is blatantly theatrical, follow the laws of nature. Their world is the rational world that we take for granted in our waking life. In it, we assume that everything that happens has a logical explanation, even if we don't always know what the explanation is.

The world of the absurd play is not logical. The usual laws simply do not apply. There is a famous play in which the characters gradually change, one after another, into rhinoceroses. An audience can accept that this can happen provided it accepts the convention within which anything can happen. This is sometimes called 'the willing suspension of disbelief' and is more common than might be expected. To a greater or lesser extent, all fiction requires it of the reader or spectator.

In the world of dreams, also, the natural laws do not apply, as you'll see if you can recall a dream you had recently. So another way of thinking of absurd plays is as though taking place in a dream world.

The playwright may use this form simply as a way of being funny, as in *Monty Python* or *Mr Bean*. But he or she may also use it to make a serious point. Do you think *Alas poor Fred* is making a serious point and, if so, what is it?

Alas poor Fred

by

James Saunders

CHARACTERS
ERNEST PRINGLE
ETHEL PRINGLE

SETTING
A drawing room anywhere.

TIME
Any time of day or night.

(ERNEST **sits in his easy chair, head back, eyes closed. In the other easy chair** ETHEL **knits. All is peace.**)

ERNEST   I can't get over poor Fred . . . It seems like only yesterday.

(Pause)

ETHEL   It must be funny to be cut in half . . .

ERNEST   He wouldn't have thought so. But he was never of course blessed with what you might call a sense of humour.

ETHEL   He was a good man.

ERNEST   I'll grant you that. All I'm saying –

ETHEL   A Christian. He went to church regularly. Every Christmas day.

ERNEST   Granted, Ethel, but –

ETHEL   Whatever you say about him you can't deny this: he always kept his moustache straight. It says a lot for a man.

ERNEST   Moustache? What moustache?

ETHEL   His moustache.

ERNEST   Fred?

ETHEL   Fred.

ERNEST   Fred had no moustache.

ETHEL   You're saying he was clean-shaven?

ERNEST   If you like to put it like that.

ETHEL   I don't know how you can sit there and look me in the eye –

ERNEST   If Fred had a moustache, what about the photograph of him on the promenade at Sandwich in 1935? Hey? Answer me that.

(Pause)

ETHEL   He never went to Sandwich.

ERNEST   Are you sitting there in that chair –

ETHEL   Winchelsea. Rye. Not Sandwich. He disliked Sandwich.

ERNEST   How could he dislike Sandwich if he never went there?

ETHEL   He disliked the name. He'd never even eat a sandwich, let alone go to Sandwich.

ERNEST   My dear Ethel, ham sandwiches were his favourite food!

ETHEL   Ham. Not sandwiches.

ERNEST   Ethel, in 1935, at Sandwich, in the company of yourself and myself, Fred had his photograph taken while eating a ham sandwich.

ETHEL   No. Deal perhaps. 1934 perhaps. Eating a roll. With Tom. Not Fred.

ERNEST   We shall see about that.

(He fetches a box of photographs.)

ERNEST   Now . . .

(He looks through the photographs.)

Where the devil are my glasses?

ETHEL   You've got them on, dear.

ERNEST   What? Ah yes, that's better . . .

(He finds a photograph.)

Ah! Now! See here! Look at this photograph!

(He hands it to ETHEL.**)**

See. Yourself. Myself. Fred. Eating a ham sandwich. Clean-shaven. Now look at the back. What does it say? 'The promenade, Sandwich, 1935.' The promenade, Sandwich, 1935.

(He turns the photograph over and over to make his point.)

Yourself. Myself. Fred. No moustache. Ham sandwich. The promenade, Sandwich, 1935, Fred, yourself, myself. Clean-shaven. Ham sandwich, 1935. The promenade, Sandwich. Fred. No moustache. Ham sandwich.

(ERNEST **returns victoriously to his chair, and closes his eyes. Pause.**)

ETHEL   If it were.

ERNEST   If it were what?

ETHEL   If it were Fred.

ERNEST   If what were Fred?

ETHEL   If it were Fred.

(ERNEST **gets up and snatches the photograph away.**)

ERNEST   If that isn't Fred then who the devil is it?

ETHEL   Bill.

ERNEST   Bill who?

ETHEL   Bill Quink.

ERNEST   But Bill Quink had a moustache. This man is clean-shaven.

ETHEL   No, dear. Bill Quink was clean-shaven. Sam Quink had a moustache.

(ERNEST **jumps to his feet.**)

ERNEST   Am I to be master in my own house or not! One minute you promise to love, honour and obey me and the next minute you contradict my every word! I've had enough of it, do you hear? Your cousin's husband is a mannerless pig, and your mother's aunt has no taste in hats! I'm going to take Fido for a walk!

(**He goes out.**)

ETHEL   Fido died three years ago. In any case his name was Susie. She was a bitch . . .

(ERNEST **returns.**)

ERNEST   I decided against it . . . I went for a walk yesterday, when all's said and done. I don't like to get into habits . . . In any case, Fido is not fond of walking, you know.

(**He sits down.**)

Not since she died . . .

(Pause)

ETHEL   If he had any weakness at all it was this: that he was not blessed with what you might call a sense of humour.

ERNEST   Oh, I don't know. After all, to be cut in half is no joke. I mean, if you're the one who's cut in half.

ETHEL   But Ernest, even before he was cut in half he still didn't have what you might call a sense of humour.

ERNEST   You mean being cut in half made no difference.

ETHEL   Exactly.

ERNEST   Yes, I see your point . . . So in that case, why was he cut in half in the first place?

ETHEL   But Ernest, you did it yourself.

ERNEST   I know that, Ethel, that is not the point at issue. The question is not who but why. Why did I cut Fred in half?

ETHEL   It was being in the wardrobe, you see.

ERNEST   Wardrobe? Fred?

ETHEL   You. Cast off one stitch and continue . . .

ERNEST   I've never been in a wardrobe in my life. Why would I be in a wardrobe?

ETHEL   On account of Fred.

ERNEST   On account of Fred I was in my wardrobe?

ETHEL   Fred's.

ERNEST   What?

ETHEL   Wardrobe.

ERNEST   I was in Fred's wardrobe?

ETHEL   Yes. Cast off one stitch and continue . . .

ERNEST   Doing what, may I ask?

ETHEL   Hiding.

ERNEST   From whom?

ETHEL   Fred.

ERNEST   Ethel, correct me if I'm wrong, but it seems to me that if I wished to hide from Fred, then I should hide not in his wardrobe but in my own.

ETHEL   You had no wardrobe of your own.

ERNEST   I've got one upstairs.

ETHEL   This was then.

ERNEST   So where was this famous wardrobe I was hiding in?

ETHEL   Upstairs.

ERNEST   Upstairs? There's no wardrobe upstairs. I mean there's my wardrobe. Not Fred's.

ETHEL   But it was.

ERNEST   What?

ETHEL   The wardrobe.

ERNEST   What?

ETHEL   Fred's.

ERNEST   My wardrobe was Fred's? You mean he gave it to me?

ETHEL   Not gave.

ERNEST   Then what?

ETHEL   It was after he was cut in half.

ERNEST   That he gave me his – Wait. I see. Not gave. Took. I was hiding in Fred's wardrobe. Then I cut him in half. Then I took his wardrobe. Is that why I cut him in half? To take his wardrobe?

ETHEL   You didn't take it.

ERNEST   Then who the devil did?

ETHEL   No one. It stayed there.

ERNEST   I don't think you quite follow my line of reasoning. Fred had a wardrobe. In his house –

ETHEL   But Ernest, this was Fred's house.

ERNEST   But this is my house!

ETHEL   It was Fred's house.

ERNEST   My house was Fred's? Are you sure?

ETHEL   Yes, Ernest.

ERNEST   Very well, then. Let's recapitulate. I am hiding in the wardrobe. Enter Fred, with or without his moustache. He finds me in the wardrobe, I cut him in half. Because he found me in the – Ah! No! This is it! Listen. This was the trouble. He didn't laugh, did he?

ETHEL   When you cut him in half?

ERNEST   No, no, when he found me in the wardrobe. If he'd laughed, if he'd seen the funny side of it, things might have turned out quite differently. It wasn't as if he knew he was going to be cut in half.

ETHEL   That's true.

ERNEST   Is that why I did it? Because he didn't laugh?

ETHEL   You hate being laughed at.

ERNEST   Not at, Ethel. With. I'm talking about with. Laughed with.

ETHEL   Only he didn't have what you might call –

ERNEST   Exactly. And paid the penalty . . . One thing puzzles me. While I was hiding in Fred's wardrobe and Fred was coming in and finding me and I was cutting him in half – where were you?

ETHEL   In bed, Ernest.

ERNEST   In bed? But I always go to bed before you. If you were in bed, what was I doing in the wardrobe?

ETHEL   You got up again.

ERNEST   What for?

ETHEL   To hide in the wardrobe.

ERNEST   Yes, I see . . . No, wait! There's a discrepancy. There's a flaw in the logic of this somewhere. You were in bed. Correct?

ETHEL   Yes.

ERNEST   I also was in bed . . . The same bed?

ETHEL   Yes.

ERNEST   Now. I got out of bed. I hid in the wardrobe. Fred found me in the wardrobe. You were in bed. Now, answer me this: Who let Fred in?

ETHEL   But Ernest, he let himself in.

ERNEST   Self? How, self? He comes to our house –

ETHEL   It was his house.

ERNEST   Ah, yes, I'd forgotten. Yes, that explains – No, wait! Ethel, what are you saying?

ETHEL   Would you care for a glass of hot milk?

ERNEST   If this was Fred's house, Ethel, what were we doing in bed in it?

(Pause)

ETHEL   Perhaps we were tired.

ERNEST   Come now, Ethel. If we were tired, why didn't we go home to bed?

ETHEL   I was home.

ERNEST   Do pay attention, Ethel. This was Fred's house, we've arrived at that. So how could you –

ETHEL   I was Fred's wife.

ERNEST   Fred's? But Ethel, you're my wife. I'm almost certain of that. You're married to me, you've always been married to me.

ETHEL   Nearly always.

ERNEST   So if . . . But if . . . Ethel, if you were Fred's wife, what . . . ?

(He stops, lost in thought. Pause.)

ETHEL   We were lovers . . . We were lovers, Ernest . . .

(ERNEST is engrossed in his meditation.)

Ernest, we were lovers . . . Lovers . . . Lovers . . .

(Pause. She knits quietly.)

How is it, I wonder, that one can be one thing, then a completely different thing?

ERNEST   Well, well, it's all a mystery, that's all I can say. That's my honest opinion. A mystery . . .

(He rests his head back and closes his eyes. She knits.)

The end

Tricking the Trickster

Melodrama

Melodramas exaggerate. Although what happens in this play is possible, it is not very probable. Performance helps an audience to accept the improbable; if the action moves fast enough, there is little time to ask questions. Do you think you can make what happens in this play convincing? It is a question once again of the 'willing suspension of disbelief' and here much depends on visual illusion: the strange room, candlelight, thunder and lightning, Mary's white dress, the sword . . . The incidents are intended to be sensational, like Dave's hasty exit. Can they also be frightening?

The characters, too, are exaggerated. They are stereotypes: the misunderstood hero, the wronged heroine, the heartless villain, the faithful servant. If you watch soap operas on television, you may well recognise some of them. The audience is expected to take sides: in the Victorian theatre, it used to hiss and boo the villain.

If a play or situation is exaggerated beyond the point of credibility, it is called melodramatic. The word is often used as a criticism. Are there elements in *Tricking the Trickster* which stop it going 'over the top'? Are the characters crudely portrayed as black or white, as in a morality play, or are they credible? What about the humour? The ending is happy but not in the usual way. Is it what you expected?

Tricking the Trickster
by
Robin Rook

CHARACTERS
ROGER KNOWLES, an octogenarian historian
MARY, his great-niece
DAVE, her boyfriend
MARTHA, the elderly housekeeper

SETTING
Knowles' study on the first floor of a large Victorian house in
North Oxford. It is cluttered with the paraphernalia of his
profession. A sword in the fireplace is used as a poker.
Everything is dilapidated, the window obscured with ivy.
Very neo-Gothic.

TIME
Late afternoon in winter.

Note: Knollys in the text is pronounced like Knowles.

Scene 1

(MARY **is warming herself at the fire,** MARTHA **is looking
out of the window.**)

MARTHA   Nice young man you got there.

MARY   **(Smiling)** Not that young, Martha. He's nearly sixteen years
older than me.

MARTHA   Rum lot, you Knowles: first your grandad goes and marries
what he called a flapper, then your mum runs off with a man
twice her age and now the professor gets tangled up with a
hussy he's never even met . . .

MARY   She's been dead for hundreds of years.

MARTHA   Doesn't stop him rummaging about in her past like a jealous
lover, does it? Says she was wronged . . .

MARY   Is he still infatuated with her?

MARTHA	Worse than ever. Talks of nothing else. Mal this and Mal that. She's as real to him as you or me.
MARY	Oh, dear. I thought he might grow out of it.
MARTHA	After all this time? It started before you were born.
MARY	**(Smiling)** I wouldn't know about that.
MARTHA	Why do you think you was called Mary? Or perhaps you know...
MARY	I've no idea.
MARTHA	After her.
MARY	Really?
MARTHA	He said he would leave everything to you if you was christened Mary.
MARY	And Mother agreed?
MARTHA	Must have, mustn't she? You don't have no other name.
MARY	No, I don't.
MARTHA	Everything. This house, his books, what's left of the family fortune . . .
MARY	He will make provision for you.
MARTHA	Wouldn't think so. You're his little Mal and it's all yours.

(DAVE **appears silently in the door.**)

MARY	Don't worry, Martha. If he's really left everything to me, when the time comes I'll see you're taken care of.
MARTHA	'Course you will. I'll be all you have left, won't I, my little pigeon?
DAVE	**(Coming into the room.)** Not quite all, Martha. You'll have me to reckon with then.
MARY	Martha was just saying how much she likes you.
DAVE	**(Smiling)** She'd better or she might find herself missing out.
MARY	**(Laughing)** Oh, Dave, how can you say such a thing? Martha's one of the family.
DAVE	That makes four of us.
MARY	Once we're engaged.

DAVE   I thought we would announce it tonight. After dinner, here in the study. Make it official.

MARY   What a lovely idea.

DAVE   Give the old boy a treat.

MARTHA   A shock more like.

DAVE   What's that meant to mean?

MARTHA   If he's normal I dare say it'll be all right but if he's in one of his moods . . .

MARY   We must take care he doesn't drink too much.

MARTHA   That too. His heart's not what it was.

MARY   Has he been to the doctor?

MARTHA   Not him. But I know.

MARY   He really should.

MARTHA   Try telling him. Quacks he calls them and some other name.

MARY   Mountebanks?

MARTHA   That's it. He doesn't live in the present no more. It's all that reading – never did anyone no good.

MARY   It's his life, Martha.

MARTHA   It'll be his death if he don't watch out.

DAVE   He's had a good run for his money. And if I'm any judge he's got a few more miles left in him.

MARY   (Smiling) You always look on the bright side, darling.

DAVE   It's the job. Spend all day persuading punters that old bangers are really kosher and you can't wipe the smirk off your face. It becomes a fixture.

MARY   It will be easier once you have your own business.

DAVE   That's up to you, isn't it?

MARY   You know I want nothing else.

DAVE   Sure you do. And if we were alone, I'd show my appreciation.

MARY   Dave!

DAVE   (Joining her at the fireplace.) That's new.

MARY   What is?

DAVE   The poker.

MARY   I was wondering what it was for.

DAVE   Only an oddball like your uncle would use a sword.

MARTHA   He says it's not a firearm but the next best thing.

MARY   He likes riddles.

DAVE   Where is he anyway? He knew we were coming.

MARTHA   At the Bodleian. Where else would he be?

DAVE   And what's that when it's at home?

MARY   The University library.

MARTHA   World famous.

DAVE   Not in my world, it's not! **(He laughs.)**

MARY   Scholars do get rather self-centred.

DAVE   Stuck up, I call it.

MARY   Uncle's not like that. He doesn't despise people who are . . .

DAVE   Ignorant?

MARY   Less well-informed.

DAVE   I bet he doesn't know the difference between a gearbox and a crankshaft.

MARY   He's never owned a car.

DAVE   How does he get around – on horseback?

MARY   You know perfectly well – on his bicycle. He calls it Rosinante after Don Quixote's horse.

DAVE   Another bloody riddle.

MARY   You got on so well with him last time . . .

DAVE   And do you know for why? Because I mended that puncture. He thought I was the bee's knees – even if he did mistake me for a blacksmith!

MARY   Does it really matter so long as he likes you?

DAVE   It doesn't, so long as you do.

MARY   Oh, Dave . . .

MARTHA   (**Looking out of the window.**) He's down there now pushing that contraption of his. Another opportunity for you, Mr Dutton, to get in his good books, I wouldn't wonder.

DAVE   He'll only try and put me down.

MARY   He wouldn't do it on purpose.

DAVE   Only joking, silly.

ROGER   (**Off-stage**) Martha! Have they arrived yet?

MARTHA   (**At the door.**) In the study, sir.

ROGER   (**Off-stage**) Damned horse went lame. I'm coming up.

MARY   Offer to mend it.

DAVE   You bet.

MARY   Don't upset him. Remember it's our engagement day.

DAVE   I'm not likely to forget.

   (**Enter** ROGER. **His manner is theatrical.**)

ROGER   There you are, my precious Mal. I've been reading about you all the afternoon in those letters I wrote to your sister. She must have shown them to you. Why else would she have kept them? (**Quoting**) 'My eyes see what I cannot attain to, my ears hear what I do scant believe, and my thoughts are carried with contrary conceits . . . ' Remember?

MARY   I have no sister, Uncle.

ROGER   And my name is not William. Why was I christened Roger? A ludicrous name fit only for bawdy. I shall not forgive my parents, God rest their souls. But you are Mary and I am Knowles. You bear the name of the incomparable Mistress Fitton and I cannot but be descended from the woebegone Sir William Knollys. We are the incarnation of that great passion, debarred now by bonds of blood as once we were by ties of wedlock. You have the very likeness of Mal and I the hoary age of Sir William. Is it not fitting, think you?

MARY   I think you have been over-exerting yourself.

ROGER   The words still dance before my eyes like the dying embers of that fire. (**Leading her to the fire.**) Come, warm yourself beside them before they are extinguished quite. (**Coming face to face with** DAVE.) And who are you?

MARY   You must remember Dave, Uncle. He mended your bicycle last time we stayed.

ROGER   And so he shall again. Welcome, faithful Dave. I am glad to see you well.

DAVE   Cheers.

ROGER   Martha, this is a time for celebration. You have killed the fatted calf, no?

MARTHA   No. It's lamb.

ROGER   No matter. We must choose wine to match your peerless cooking. Excuse me, Niece, we must visit the cellar. **(To DAVE.)** Shall I see you at dinner, sir?

DAVE   I'm invited.

ROGER   Good, good. Come, Martha. I wasted time, and now doth time waste me!

(He exits laughing, followed by MARTHA.)

MARY   Oh Dave, he's so much worse.

DAVE   Stark staring bonkers!

MARY   What can we do?

DAVE   Play along with him. If he thinks you're this Mal Fitton, then Mal Fitton you must be.

MARY   Ought we to encourage him?

DAVE   If he wants it, why not?

MARY   I suppose you're right.

DAVE   I know I'm right. So when we announce our engagement you must appear as her.

MARY   How can I do that?

DAVE   You know that old dress he keeps in one of the spare rooms . . .

MARY   The white one?

DAVE   He thinks it belonged to her, doesn't he?

MARY   But it's only a figment of his imagination.

DAVE   Real for him. After dinner, when we come here for the port, you go and put it on.

MARY   What if it doesn't fit?

DAVE   Get Martha to give you a hand.

MARY   But . . .

DAVE   It'll really send him to see you dressed in it.

MARY   You think so?

DAVE   Wasn't she seduced?

MARY   Yes.

DAVE   And the bloke refused to marry her?

MARY   Yes.

DAVE   There you are. That's the difference. We're going to get married. Think how chuffed he'll be if the story has a happy ending.

MARY   I don't know . . .

DAVE   My name is Dutton. You'll become Mary Dutton. Even closer to the original. He'll love it.

MARY   If I could be sure . . .

DAVE   Don't you trust me?

MARY   Of course I do.

DAVE₀   Then take my word for it.

(A faint flash of lightning and a distant roll of thunder.)

MARY   There's going to be a storm.

DAVE   It was forecast.

MARY   I'm frightened.

DAVE   Come here, you idiot, it's only an electrical fault in the sky, something shorting somewhere.

MARY   Dave darling, comfort me.

(He holds her in his arms.)

DAVE   Better?

MARY   Yes.

DAVE   And you'll do what I say? (MARY **nods.**) That's my girl.

Scene 2

> (**Later that night. The study is lit by a single reading lamp on the desk and by the occasional flash of lightning from the window. The storm is nearer.**)
>
> (MARTHA **enters with the port and goes to draw the curtains. Enter** ROGER.)

ROGER   Leave them, Martha. God's light is better than man's.

MARTHA   Very good, sir.

ROGER   (**Quietly**) They'll be here soon?

MARTHA   (**Quietly**) Any minute.

ROGER   We must be on our guard. (**Aloud**) A splendid dinner. You excelled yourself.

MARTHA   The young people enjoyed it.

ROGER   Who wouldn't at their age when the blood runs hot in the veins? They have a lusty appetite.

MARTHA   Yours isn't so bad.

ROGER   (**Poking the fire.**) Unrequited . . . unrequited . . .

MARTHA   Mind you go easy on the port.

ROGER   (**Laughing**) Do you take me for a drunkard?

MARTHA   You have been known to overdo it.

ROGER   To assuage my solitude. Tonight I have company.

MARTHA   They'll not thank you if you get maudlin.

ROGER   Banish the thought.

MARTHA   (**Looking towards the door.**) They make a handsome couple.

ROGER   A look of the Earl, don't you think?

MARTHA   What Earl?

ROGER   Pembroke, of course. (**Quietly to** MARTHA.) Mal's seducer. (**Aloud**) William Herbert. Mr W H, Shakespeare's only begetter.

MARTHA   At your riddles again.

ROGER   Plain as a pikestaff. You can smile and smile and still be a villain. Set it down, Martha, set it down.

MARTHA   If you're going to take on, I'll be leaving you.

ROGER   Prepare candles as you go. They'll withstand the storm better than these new-fangled lights.

MARTHA   **(Quietly)** He's coming. **(Aloud)** That's the first sensible thing . . .

ROGER   About your business, chatterbox.

(She exits. ROGER pours himself a glass of port.)

ROGER   **(Holding the glass to the light.)** Pure nectar.

(Enter DAVE.)

DAVE   **(Cheerfully)** Hang about! There's others wouldn't mind joining in.

ROGER   Help yourself.

DAVE   **(Doing so.)** Good stuff if it's the same as last time.

ROGER   Nothing is ever the same as last time.

DAVE   Improves with age.

ROGER   Don't we all? **(Proposing a toast.)** To our sovereign lady, Elizabeth.

DAVE   Cheers.

ROGER   Where's Mal?

DAVE   In the girls' room.

ROGER   The Coffer Chamber.

DAVE   What?

ROGER   Where the Maids of Honour retire.

DAVE   Wouldn't know about that, I stick to the gents'.

ROGER   I went there once, foolish, fond old man that I was.

DAVE   I hope for your sake it was empty.

ROGER   Crowded. They were all there.

DAVE   Bloody hell.

ROGER   I was reading a book . . .

DAVE   Bit of a liberty.

ROGER   . . . dressed in my night-gown . . .

DAVE   Must have scared the daylights out of them.

ROGER   But that was before your time, before you came to Court.

DAVE   Glad to hear it.

ROGER   **(Looking out of the window.)** Just such a stormy night.

(Lightning)

DAVE   We've got a little announcement to make . . .

ROGER   **(Suspiciously)** Again?

DAVE   We've not told anyone else.

ROGER   Then why me?

DAVE   You'll be pleased.

ROGER   You think so?

DAVE   Certain. It's a bit of a surprise.

ROGER   Surprise?

DAVE   Mary wants to tell you herself.

ROGER   Does she now? **(Distractedly)** Echoes . . . voices from the past . . . always the same . . . the same . . . Damnation!

(Thunder)

DAVE   After all, she is your Mal.

ROGER   She is my cross, yet I needs must love her.

DAVE   And she loves you. **(Smiling)** More than me, and that's saying something.

ROGER   **(Violently)** Don't tell me, you man of sin!

DAVE   **(Nervously)** Steady on. We've not done nothing we shouldn't. Ask her.

ROGER   She shall speak for herself.

DAVE   That's what I said.

ROGER   I care not what you say. Perjurer!

DAVE   What about another drink?

ROGER   Never.

DAVE   A top up?

ROGER   Out of my sight!

(He pushes past DAVE **to the fire. Brilliant flash of light-**
ning. The desk lamp goes out. MARY **appears in the door**
in the white dress holding a candle.)

ROGER   **(Seeing her.)** No. No! Not chaste! Not white! No maid! Don't
torment me.

MARY   We only wanted to tell you . . .

ROGER   **(Picking up the 'poker.')** You have betrayed me. Betrayed
my love, my honour, my good name!

MARY   Uncle, please . . .

ROGER   **(Moving towards her.)** Too late! Your prayers are spent.
They move me not.

MARY   **(Terrified)** Dave!

DAVE   Put it down, you old fool.

ROGER   I'll not harm you, Mal, nor mar that skin smooth as monumental
alabaster. You have brought ruin on yourself. But I'll protect you
still. Still! How can I? **(In tears.)** Too late . . . too late . . .

DAVE   Tell him.

MARY   We are going to be married.

ROGER   Married!

MARY   Dave and I.

ROGER   Marry with that villain?

MARY   We love each other.

ROGER   Blind. Blind! Can you not see he's false?

DAVE   Come off it.

MARY   He loves me. Tell him, Dave.

ROGER   **(Threatening** DAVE **with the sword.)** Tell me. If you dare!

DAVE   Well, you see, we thought it would be nice if we got married
while you're still here to give her away . . .

ROGER   Give her away! I'd sooner kill you first, you loathsome toad!

DAVE   **(Backing towards the window.)** Just an idea, nothing
serious, it can wait . . .

MARY   **(Shocked)** Dave.

ROGER   It can wait till the seas run dry and the mountains are level with the plains. **(Advancing on** DAVE.**)** It can wait till villains keep their word and maids are not abused. I'll show you how long it can wait!

(He lunges at DAVE **who scrambles through the window.)**

MARY   Stop it, Uncle, stop it!

(Thunder. A cry as DAVE **falls.)**

MARY   You've killed him!

ROGER   **(Suddenly sober and collected.)** Killed him? Fat chance of that. It's only a few feet to the ground.

(He replaces the 'poker'. MARY **goes to the window.)**

MARY   Thank God. He's all right.

ROGER   Heading for the car, no doubt.

MARY   He's getting into it.

ROGER   Safest place. So much for Master Dave.

MARY   What do you mean?

ROGER   Couldn't you see he was a rotter?

MARY   Uncle . . .

ROGER   No use telling you, you wouldn't have listened. It was obvious to Martha and me last time you came. **(Calling at the door.)** Martha, you can put the lights back on.

MARY   Martha knew?

ROGER   From the start. His reaction to the news of your inheritance merely confirmed her suspicions.

MARY   You mean the whole thing was put on?

(The desk lamp comes on.)

ROGER   That's better. I can see to pour the port. We've got something to celebrate now.

MARY   You made it all up?

ROGER   **(Laughing)** With a bit of help from the Bard. **(Filling two glasses.)** I've been researching into Mal Fitton's extraordinary affair with Knollys off and on for thirty years. I daresay it's become a bit of an obsession. But it came in handy this time, didn't it? Instead of me dropping dead from a heart attack at the sight of you dressed as Mal, it put paid to Master Dave's little game. **(Laughing)** Hoist with his own petard!

MARY   Uncle, you of all people . . .

ROGER   **(Handing** MARY **a glass of port.)** Always fancied myself as a bit of an actor. Wish I'd been around in Shakespeare's time. Shall we drink to that?

MARY   But, Uncle . . .

ROGER   **(Raising his glass.)** It's twice the fun to trick the trickster. In his very own words: Cheers!

The end

Short Notice

The primary purpose of farce is to amuse. Easily recognisable characters find themselves in awkward or embarrassing situations. Chance and human error lead to rapidly changing circumstances. The basic plot of *Short Notice* is very simple: it needs constant twists in the action to keep it going. Can you spot these?

In performance it is essential that the action moves fast. The audience must not be given time to stop and think, it must be carried along from one ridiculous situation to the next. It is always kept 'in the know' so it can enjoy the confusion and the way actors talk at cross-purposes. The more seriously the actors behave, the funnier they will be.

The characters in *Short Notice* are pretentious, they want to keep up a social front. Part of the fun is watching this being put at risk and their desperate attempts to keep it intact. They are easy to portray and the comedy lies in the unfolding situation, but it needs considerable skill to act successfully. It depends on split-second timing. Nothing can be left to chance or else the whole elaborate structure will fall to pieces. What would happen if an actor failed to enter on cue? The slightest delay would put belief in the situation at risk. It is a real challenge to keep the audience involved throughout.

But although involved, the audience must be kept 'at arm's length'; it must not be allowed to sympathise with the characters on stage. Sympathy kills laughter. For instance, if a pompous man slips on a banana skin it is funny. We laugh at his loss of face; he had it coming to him. But if he were to break his leg, he would cease to be an object of fun and become a subject for pity. Situations can build to the brink of disaster but they must not become disastrous. How is this avoided in *Short Notice*?

Short Notice
by
Robin Rook

CHARACTERS
PETER JONES
JANE, his wife
MICHAEL ROBERTS
MYRA, his wife

SETTING
The kitchen of the Joneses, who try to live up to their name.

TIME
A Sunday evening in February.

(JANE is making sandwiches. Enter PETER in his dressing gown.)

PETER   The bathroom's free. I'll make the coffee.

JANE   Big deal.

PETER   What do you mean, 'big deal'?

JANE   Making the coffee while I slave away at supper.

PETER   Sandwiches hardly constitute supper.

JANE   What else would you call them?

PETER   A snack, a nibble, a gobbet . . .

JANE   Don't be disgusting.

PETER   I refrained from saying titbit.

JANE   I should hope so.

PETER   Not that it has anything to do with that.

JANE   With what?

PETER   A bit of tit.

JANE   Peter! Amanda might hear.

PETER   She's asleep.

JANE   You never know.

PETER   I peered in on the way down. Anyway, not even I know where titbit comes from.

JANE   Look it up. You usually do.

PETER   I believe in self-improvement.

         (He exits.)

JANE   I've nearly finished these.

PETER   **(Off-stage)** You'd better hurry if you want a bath.

JANE   What time is it?

PETER   **(Off-stage)** Nearly half seven.

JANE   Plenty of time.

PETER   **(Off-stage)** Is there?

JANE   It doesn't start till eight.

         (PETER **returns with the Concise Oxford Dictionary.)**

PETER   It didn't used to.

JANE   Heaps of time.

PETER   Not tonight.

JANE   Why not?

PETER   Because it starts at a quarter to.

JANE   How can it?

PETER   They've brought it forward because of the Peckham disaster. An extended news.

JANE   I might have known. No bath! And it's all your fault.

PETER   The Peckham disaster?

JANE   Not telling me sooner.

PETER   I thought you knew. Here we are. **(Reading)** 'Titbit: Perhaps from dialect *tid*, tender plus bit.' I dare say it is.

JANE   For goodness' sake, Peter, get out of my way.

PETER   You asked me to look it up.

JANE   That doesn't mean you can monopolise the kitchen.

PETER   Nothing could be further from my thoughts.

JANE   Selfish brute.

PETER   Touchy!

JANE   I know, I know. It's been a long hard weekend, and I was looking forward to that bath.

        (PETER **exits.**)

PETER   If you miss the first bit, I can always fill you in.

JANE   And ruin the rest of it? No thank you.

PETER   **(Off-stage)** Some day we'll get a video.

JANE   You've been saying that for years.

PETER   **(Off-stage)** You know perfectly well it was a straight choice – Amanda or the video, double-glazing and a second car.

JANE   No choice at all.

PETER   **(Off-stage)** Not for you. Though I must admit . . . Good Lord!

JANE   What now?

PETER   **(Off-stage)** They're coming to the door.

JANE   Who are?

PETER   **(Off-stage)** Michael and Myra.

JANE   **(Disbelieving)** Who?

PETER   **(Off-stage)** Our friends, Michael and Myra Roberts.

JANE   I know perfectly well who they are . . . They can't be!

PETER   **(Off-stage)** Dressed to kill.

JANE   Let me see **(She exits. Pause. Screeching)** You're right. It is!

PETER   **(Off-stage)** Get back in the kitchen. They'll see us.

JANE   **(Off-stage)** Why didn't you draw the curtains?

PETER   **(Off-stage)** Why didn't you?

        (JANE **enters followed by** PETER.)

JANE   What on earth can they want?

PETER   **(Joking)** Perhaps they're coming to dinner . . . No!

JANE   Impossible!

(They make a concerted dash for the kitchen calendar.)

PETER   Let me see. I'm quicker.

JANE   Not without your glasses, you're not.

PETER   Well?

JANE   Sunday, twenty-ninth February . . .

PETER   It would be a leap year.

JANE   What's that got to do with it?

PETER   One day too many.

JANE   Twenty ninth Feb. It is today, isn't it?

PETER   Of course it's today. Sunday. The night for 'Westenders'.

JANE   Nothing.

PETER   Nothing?

JANE   Nothing.

PETER   Drawn a blank. Jolly good.

JANE   They must be on their way somewhere else.

PETER   Coming up our path?

JANE   You know how forgetful they are.

PETER   They're not in the least forgetful. Quite the opposite in fact . . .

(The door bell chimes. PETER and JANE 'freeze' in horror.)

JANE   **(Hoarsely)** It's them.

PETER   Must be.

JANE   What do they want?

PETER   No idea, but it's their mistake.

JANE   Positive?

PETER   We just looked.

JANE   True.

PETER   We'll have to tell them.

JANE   We can't.

PETER   What else can we do?

JANE   We absolutely can't.

PETER   Why not?

JANE   Put yourself in their shoes.

PETER   I wish I could.

JANE   But just imagine . . .

PETER   The embarrassment.

PETER   For them.

JANE   And for us.

PETER   **(Dashed)** And for us.

(The bell chimes again.)

JANE   We'll have to answer.

PETER   I know! Let's pretend we're out. Then they'll go home, look at their diary and discover it's their mistake. Phew! What a relief.

JANE   Just one snag.

PETER   What?

JANE   You put the lights on when you left the sitting room.

PETER   So I did.

JANE   And lights don't just go on.

PETER   No, they don't.

JANE   Someone has to put them on.

PETER   That's right. Us.

JANE   One of us. You, you great berk!

PETER   Whoever.

JANE   Well, it wasn't me, was it?

PETER   Not this time.

JANE   You mean they're going to make a habit of coming to dinner uninvited?

PETER   They'll never come again if we keep them waiting much longer.

JANE   Answer the door then.

PETER   Like this?

JANE	No, I suppose not. But don't just stand there. Go and get dressed.
PETER	They'll see me going upstairs. The fanlight, you know.
JANE	You'll just have to stay here.
PETER	All night?
JANE	Till I take them into the sitting room.
PETER	But it's open plan.
JANE	I know it's open plan! I'll take them to the back window, point out something in the garden . . .
PETER	How'll I know?
JANE	What?
PETER	When the coast is clear.
JANE	I'll say, 'Aren't they lovely'.
PETER	Good. **(Repeating)** 'Aren't they lovely?' Got it.
JANE	Right. Here goes.
PETER	Good luck.

(JANE **exits.** PETER **skulks. The front door is opened. The ensuing dialogue takes place off-stage.)**

JANE	Hello there. Lovely to see you.
MYRA	We've been looking forward to it all week.
JANE	Don't count your chickens.
MYRA	You're such a marvellous cook. Never a disaster.
JANE	There's always a first . . .
MICHAEL	Nonsense, Jane. How are you?
JANE	Fine, thank you, Michael.
MYRA	He's brought flowers. When I saw them I thought they were for me. But he never remembers!
JANE	Of course, it's your wedding anniversary.
MYRA	That's why you invited us, remember?
JANE	Of course.
MICHAEL	Anyway, the flowers are for you, Jane.

JANE   Thanks so much. Aren't they lovely?

(PETER **dashes out.**)

MICHAEL   Good Lord.

JANE   Peter!

MYRA   What a surprise.

PETER   Sorry. Got rather behind . . . Took longer than I expected . . . choosing the wine . . . Special occasion, you know . . . Shan't be a tick.

JANE   I'll just put these in water. Help yourself to drinks. You know where everything is.

MYRA   I'll give you a hand.

JANE   Please don't bother, I can manage.

(**She enters, followed by** MYRA.)

MYRA   Want a word with you anyway. Michael will look after himself.

JANE   I don't know what's got into Peter. I thought he was upstairs.

MYRA   Don't worry, Jane, it doesn't matter, it doesn't really . . .

JANE   (**Putting flowers in a vase.**) He's usually so reliable.

MYRA   (**Laughing**) And look at you, all flustered, when it's us who are in a mess.

JANE   What do you mean?

MYRA   That's what I want to tell you.

(MICHAEL **peers into the kitchen.**)

MICHAEL   Mind if I put on the telly? I want to catch the opening of tonight's episode of 'Westenders'. I know we can't see it all but . . .

JANE   I don't see why not.

MICHAEL   We all know what Peter thinks about people who put telly before their friends.

JANE   Just this once. It is your anniversary.

MICHAEL   Wouldn't be fair.

JANE   We're hooked on it too.

MYRA   I don't know what you're fussing about, Michael. You know perfectly well we've arranged to see it on Brenda's video.

MICHAEL	How silly of me, I'd forgotten. Can I get you girls a drink?
MYRA	**(Pointedly)** When we've finished the flowers.
MICHAEL	Sorry, didn't mean to intrude. Just a bit lonely out here.
	(He exits.)
MYRA	In case he pops in again, I'd better tell you straight out. We're going to separate.
JANE	No, darling. How awful. Our best friends.
MYRA	Quite an occasion, I'm afraid. Hail and farewell all on the same day.
JANE	Oh, Myra.
MYRA	We mustn't let it spoil the evening, not after all your hard work. That would be too mean.
JANE	**(Sitting)** I feel sick.
MYRA	Scandal whets most people's appetite. Michael and I are ravenous.
JANE	Thanks for telling me.
MYRA	I'll call him in. 'Westenders' was only an excuse.
JANE	**(To herself.)** I'll never get over this evening.
MYRA	Don't take it too much to heart. It's been coming a long time. **(Calling)** Michael, you can join us now.
	(MICHAEL enters.)
MICHAEL	That's a relief. I hate watching something if I can't see it right through. What about a drink now?
MYRA	Why not? I've told Jane.
MICHAEL	Good show. She'll need one too then.
JANE	You can say that again.
MICHAEL	Usual?
JANE	Please.
MICHAEL	I think I can hear Peter, sounds as though he's just coming. Shall I wait for him?
JANE	**(Attempting a joke.)** If we wait for him tonight, we'll all die of dehydration!

(**Enter** PETER.)

PETER	(**Cheerfully**) I've got a surprise for you all.
MYRA	And we've got one for you.
JANE	Michael and Myra are separating.
PETER	No. You don't say. How awful.
MYRA	You'll have to remain good friends with us both – separately.
PETER	Of course, we will, of course . . .
MICHAEL	So this is our last meal together in this house.
PETER	Well, not exactly.
MYRA	Our last meal as a foursome.
PETER	That's not quite what I mean.
MICHAEL	(**Laughing**) Of course, you've got a surprise for us too!
MYRA	How exciting.
MICHAEL	Out with it.
PETER	There's not going to be dinner . . .
JANE	(**Standing**) Peter! How can you . . . ?
PETER	It's all right, Jane.
JANE	You might have consulted me first.
PETER	You weren't there to be consulted.
JANE	Scarcely my fault.
PETER	I wanted to surprise you too.
JANE	You've certainly done that!
PETER	I always intended to splash out for Michael and Myra's anniversary. All the more reason now. I've booked a table at Langtry's.
MYRA	But what about Jane's dinner?
PETER	All taken care of. Foresight, you see. Remember how I persuaded you to do a goulash, darling?
JANE	No.
PETER	(**Spelling it out.**) The other night when we were discussing the menu.

JANE	Oh, then.
PETER	Now you know why.
JANE	Do I?
PETER	I'd planned it all along. A goulash will hot up. We can have it tomorrow. I may not have given you a break from the kitchen stove tonight, but tomorrow's another day!
MYRA	How thoughtful you are, Peter. Just the difference between you and Michael.
JANE	What about Amanda?
PETER	Thought of that too. Jenny will be here by eight.
JANE	How did you persuade her at such short notice?
PETER	**(Laughing)** Double time on Sundays!
JANE	But I can't possibly go to Langtry's dressed like this.
MICHAEL	**(Jocularly)** What's good enough for us is good enough for them.
PETER	No problem. I'll go ahead with Myra and claim our table. You can follow with Michael when you're ready. All right, old man?
MICHAEL	Fine by me.
JANE	But is it quite proper, do you think?
PETER	What?
JANE	That I should be left alone to undress in the same house as Michael – *now*.
MYRA	You'll be in separate rooms.
MICHAEL	**(Laughing)** Precisely. I hadn't exactly planned to seduce you in your own little kitchen, Jane, even if it is tidier than most people's bedrooms. How you manage it beats me.
MYRA	Not a sign of cooking anywhere.
JANE	I'm naturally tidy. I can't bear a mess.
MYRA	**(Laughing)** Not like us!
JANE	I didn't mean . . .
MYRA	Of course you didn't. But you'll need a hand with the goulash. You men can go ahead and I'll sort out the kitchen while Jane changes. Where do you keep the oven gloves?

JANE   I won't hear of it . . .

PETER   Not tonight . . .

JANE   Tonight of all nights . . .

PETER   Your first night of freedom . . .

JANE   Leave it all to me . . .

PETER   Chores are definitely out.

JANE   Peter can go with you and I'll join you when I'm ready. There's really nothing to do here.

PETER   That's right. Nothing Jane can't manage by herself. Come along, you two. To Langtry's.

MICHAEL   To Langtry's then.

MYRA   If you insist.

PETER   We do, don't we, Jane?

JANE   Absolutely.

MICHAEL   See you later then.

JANE   See you.

MICHAEL   I say, what gorgeous sandwiches. Leftovers from lunch?

JANE   Sort of.

MICHAEL   Mind if I try one? I'm starving.

JANE   Help yourself.

MYRA   You'll ruin your appetite.

MICHAEL   Too bad.

MYRA   And put on weight.

MICHAEL   That's my problem – now.

MYRA   In that case, I'll have one too.

JANE   **(With mounting hysteria.)** Go ahead. Tuck in. Finish the lot! Who cares! We don't need them any more, not now we've got the goulash!

PETER   **(Trying to usher** MICHAEL **and** MYRA **out.)** Jane's upset . . . Your news . . . Shaken us both . . .

JANE   **(Thrusting the plate of sandwiches at them.)** Here. Take them. Eat them in the car. Go on. Stuff yourselves!

PETER   Best left alone when she's like this . . .

(PETER, MICHAEL **and** MYRA **exit.)**

JANE   Make sure they eat them up, Peter. Don't want any more left-overs. You might save on the bill too. Think of that!

PETER   **(Off-stage)** I'll join you in the car.

JANE   I've got a night off too. Peter's splashing out. Amazing! We'll get a video next! No more cooking for little Jane. Not tonight.

(PETER **returns.)**

PETER   No need to rub it in. You nearly ruined everything . . .

JANE   Incredible, isn't it?

PETER   What?

JANE   How a little goes a long way!

(The bell chimes.)

PETER   **(Stunned)** The bell.

JANE   That's right. The jolly old bell.

PETER   It's them!

JANE   Who this time?

PETER   Myra and Michael. They're back.

JANE   **(Sarcastically)** Having made it up, no doubt!

PETER   No, having changed their minds . . .

JANE   Talked it over in the car . . .

PETER   Decided they'd really much sooner eat here than be seen out together in public . . .

JANE   Just think of the saving for us.

PETER   And they simply adore goulash!

JANE   I can't take any more.

PETER   I'm afraid you'll have to.

(The bell chimes again.)

JANE   You go. I simply can't.

PETER   At least I'm properly dressed to receive them this time – even if you're not.

JANE   That's right, rub it in!

(PETER **exits.** JANE **walks round the kitchen, desperately fiddling with anything that comes to hand. She hears voices off and, without thinking, picks up a large kitchen knife. She backs away from the door and as a reflex action levels the knife at the expected intruders.** PETER **enters alone.**)

PETER   Good God! Have you gone mad? Put that thing down at once.

JANE   **(Putting the knife down.)** Sorry, sorry. **(Suspiciously)** Where are they?

PETER   Who?

JANE   Our so-called friends, of course.

PETER   In the car.

JANE   In the car?

PETER   Where else.

JANE   Where else indeed? **(Viciously)** In the sitting room, for instance, you great dolt!

PETER   **(Talking to her as though she were a child and surreptitiously hiding the knife.)** There, there, darling, nothing to worry about. It'll all come right in the end.

JANE   If they're not in the sitting room, where the hell are they?

PETER   **(As before.)** I told you, darling, they're in the car.

JANE   Then who rang the bloody bell?

PETER   Jenny, of course. She's just gone upstairs to say hello to Amanda. She'll be down in a minute. **(By the door.)** In fact, she's on her way down now. **(Calling through the door.)** We're in the kitchen, Jenny. Jane's waiting to see you.

JANE   **(Joining** PETER **at the door.)** Great to see you, Jenny. Thanks so much. It's really sweet of you to come at such short notice...

The end

The Old Man Who Liked Cats

Brechtian Theatre

Bertolt Brecht (1898-1956) was one of the most important influences on the drama of this century. He wrote his plays not just to tell a story about a group of characters but, above all, to draw attention to the society in which they lived. Their actions were portrayed as a reaction to their social environment. It could be said that Society was the main character in his plays.

Because the audience is asked to make judgements on the characters and their society and not just to take them at face value, various means are introduced for keeping the audience 'at arm's length' so its judgement is not clouded with sympathy. This is called the 'alienation effect'. The audience must always be made aware that it is watching a play, which then becomes a kind of parable or moral tale. The intention is to instruct, not just to entertain. Characters talk directly to the audience and are often representative of types: the Businessman, the Soldier, the Mother. The language is kept simple and direct. Songs interrupt the action; placards make announcements and film-clips illustrate points, showing that what is seen in the play is essentially relevant to the way people live.

The term 'epic theatre' is used to describe this kind of play. As in Shakespeare's plays, the action can cover a number of years and the scenes can be quite short and range over any number of locations, using minimum scenery. Perhaps you can see similarities with morality plays and even with melodramas, although in the latter, characters are never 'explained' by the society in which they live. Some of these techniques will reappear in the fantasy play.

Can you suggest where captions or songs could be added to *The Old Man Who Liked Cats* to tell the audience how it should react to what is happening? Perhaps you could invent some examples.

The Old Man Who Liked Cats
by
James Saunders

CHARACTERS
OLD MAN
his MAID
his DAUGHTER
his GRANDSON
his HOUSEKEEPER
his DOCTOR

SETTING
The old man's bedroom, his house and the house of his
widowed daughter and grandson.

TIME
Several days or weeks.

Scene One

(The OLD MAN'S **bedroom.**)

(The OLD MAN **is propped up in bed, surrounded
by his cats, which he is feeding.**)

OLD MAN   Here you are, Felix. Now, Fluff, don't push, there's enough
for everyone, let Tibbles have some nibbles. Come along
Whitey, push in or the others will have it all. Oh, you
greedy rogues! And where's Blackie and Sandy? Ah,
there you are. Help yourselves, there's enough for all and
more where that came from. Look at them, the darlings!

(**To the audience.**) I love cats as you can see. Why?
Because they're faithful, because they're loving, because
they don't steal from me; well they don't have to, I give
them all they need and more, but that's not the point.
They won't catch mice, I admit; but why should they
when they get food without having to chase it? No, I just
like cats. They'll be sorry when I'm dead. If cats could
cry, they'd cry. Because the fact is, I'm dying, yes, I'm on
my way out. And there's my dilemma: what to do with

my money, since they tell me I can't take it with me. Cats
or people. I like cats and I don't like people, so the
answer seems obvious. My pillow's bunched up again.

(He rings a bell.)

Why don't I like people? Because they're everything cats
aren't and nothing that cats are. And they smell. Cats
never smell, well, not mine, they've all been doctored so
they don't give any trouble. Even the little maid smells
sometimes, when she's been working all day and comes
to punch my pillow up, she smells of sweat, no self-
respect. Where is the girl?

(He rings the bell again.)

Still, it's a dilemma. What would the cats do with all my
money? I could leave it to the Cats' Home, they'd dine
off cream then. But what I've done to settle the question
is to set a few traps – not for mice, for people. You'll see.
There you are at last.

(The young MAID enters.)

MAID   I'm sorry, I was outside.

OLD MAN   Sunning yourself in the garden, I suppose. Your hands
are grubby.

MAID   I was bringing in some wood, I ran straight up.

OLD MAN   Punch my pillow up for me. You're the only one does it
properly, the housekeeper's hopeless. Only don't flap
your arms about while you do it.

(The MAID rearranges his pillow.)

MAID   Is that better?

OLD MAN   It'll do.

MAID   Do you want anything else?

OLD MAN   What do you have on offer?

MAID   I'm sorry, I don't understand.

OLD MAN   I'm talking English, aren't I? You want to know if I want
anything. Well, what will you give me?

MAID   Anything that's decent, sir.

OLD MAN   Is that all? You don't like me, do you?

MAID   I didn't know I had to, sir. I'll try to if you want me to.

OLD MAN   Will you be sorry when I die?

MAID   Yes.

OLD MAN   Yes, of course you will; you'll be out of a job. Now, listen. Did you open my safe as I told you?

MAID   Yes, sir.

OLD MAN   And take out the bag with the fifty crowns in?

MAID   Yes, I did that.

OLD MAN   And did you count them to make sure they were all there?

MAID   Yes.

OLD MAN   And were they?

(A pause.)

Well?

MAID   None were missing.

OLD MAN   None were missing. That's all you have to say?

MAID   Then I gave them to the housekeeper to give to the tailor to pay your debt, as you said.

OLD MAN   Quite right. I want to be straight and know where I am with everyone before I die. All right, you can go.

MAID   Yes, sir.

(The MAID **goes out.)**

OLD MAN   So much for an honest face.

Scene Two

(The house of the old man's widowed DAUGHTER **and** GRANDSON. **The** DAUGHTER **and** GRANDSON **are having an argument.)**

DAUGHTER   The old man's dying, God help him. And here you are, his only grandchild, and can't take the trouble to go round there and help to ease him out of the world nicely.

GRANDSON   What about you? You're his only child and you never set foot there.

DAUGHTER   You know how difficult he's got in the last few years, always complaining. But you're right, I blame myself for neglecting him. It's not till someone's dying that you start to see his good points. I shall go round now and ask his forgiveness, and see if there's anything he wants.

GRANDSON   What could he want? He's a rich man.

DAUGHTER   You ought to come with me.

GRANDSON   I'll go, I'll go, as soon as I've sorted out my business. I'm in a fix. Do you want to see me bankrupt?

DAUGHTER   Not again.

GRANDSON   Or even in prison. The fact is, I've been a bit rash.

DAUGHTER   With someone else's money?

GRANDSON   A client's. I thought it would make us both a packet. It was to be a surprise for him.

DAUGHTER   If you can't be honest, you might at least be clever. I'd better go now, I don't want to be too late.

(A knock on the door.)

Someone at the door. You'll have to entertain them, I'm off.

(She goes.)

GRANDSON   If it's the police I'll have no choice. Let's see.

(He peeps into the next room.)

It's the old man's maid. I wonder what she wants.

(He talks to the audience.)

She's a nice girl. I might even have married her if she hadn't been a maid. I know she's besotted with me, poor child, she's too honest to keep it out of her eyes. I wonder if she can help me. No good trying the old man on my own. He's the cause of all my trouble. If he hadn't lent me the money I wouldn't have got the taste for trying to make it breed, I might have bred cats instead, that would have pleased him. And then if he'd let me have some more when I asked him it might have pulled me out of the hole his first lot pushed me into. It's all his fault. And sitting on all that money. Lying on it now, dying on it. The worst thing of all is, I know exactly how I could get back into his good books, and it's the one thing I can't do. He sent me a letter. He said there's no-one to carry on his family name. He wants me to drop my father's name and take his, so he can die happy. How can I do that to my dead father?

(He calls out.)

Come in!

(The MAID **enters.)**

How's my poor grandfather? Is he asking for me?

MAID	No. He's the same.
GRANDSON	I'm glad you've come to see me.
MAID	Are you really?
GRANDSON	Oh yes. The fact is, I'm in a bit of a fix.
MAID	Oh, money.
GRANDSON	Yes, as usual. Only worse than usual. Will you visit me in prison?
MAID	Oh no!
GRANDSON	You won't?
MAID	You know I will. I'd do anything for you, decent or not.
GRANDSON	There's a good girl. I can't ask him for money, you see, he doesn't trust me with it. Of course I'll be rich when he dies, but that'll be too late. There must be lots of money there, in the house, it must blow about like dust –
MAID	You're not asking me to steal for you?
GRANDSON	Would you if I did?
MAID	I don't know . . .
GRANDSON	No, what I had in mind was that you ask him for some yourself. He must like you. If you say it's urgent.
MAID	How?
GRANDSON	I don't know, say you're – pregnant and you have to get rid of it.
MAID	I can't lie. I'm no good at it.

GRANDSON	Well there isn't time to make it true! Anything, then, but just ask him. Will you do that? For me?
MAID	How much do you need?
GRANDSON	Fifty crowns.
MAID	How odd. That's why I've come to see you; to ask your advice about fifty crowns. You know about these things, you can tell me what to do.
GRANDSON	You've stolen fifty crowns?
MAID	No. Listen. He told me to get a bag out of the safe and count it. He said it had fifty crowns in. Then I was to give it to the housekeeper to pay the tailor.
GRANDSON	And you kept it.
MAID	No. I took it out and counted it, but it wasn't fifty, it was a hundred.
GRANDSON	You kept fifty back and gave the rest to the housekeeper. And the old man will never miss it. Thank God for His providence! Where is it?
MAID	I gave it all to the housekeeper.
GRANDSON	You – ! Oh, you poor innocent child! Now she'll pocket it! Did she tell you to keep quiet about it?
MAID	Yes, she said she'd take care of it.
GRANDSON	You bet she will. Well, we must make the best of a bad job. Tell the old man the housekeeper's stolen some money from him, that'll show him what an honest girl you are, he might even give you a reward. Then, when he's in the right mood, ask him for the loan of the fifty crowns.
MAID	But that's what I wanted to ask your advice about. Because if I do tell him, she'll lose her job. Jobs aren't easy to find. She might even go to prison.
GRANDSON	So she should! She's stolen fifty crowns!
MAID	But you said yourself he won't miss it. And how can I ruin her life for taking the money when I nearly took it myself?
GRANDSON	You did?
MAID	I thought about it. Who wouldn't? With fifty crowns I could set up in a little shop and only have my own floor to scrub.

GRANDSON   So why the devil didn't you?

MAID   I don't know.

GRANDSON   You don't know much, do you? All right then, keep the housekeeper out of prison. I'll go instead.

MAID   No!

GRANDSON   You can't have it both ways. No, wait, I've got an idea. Don't tell him, don't talk to her. I'll fix it.

MAID   What are you going to do?

GRANDSON   Never you mind.

Scene Three

(The OLD MAN's **house.**)

(The HOUSEKEEPER **talks to the audience.**)

HOUSEKEEPER   It's not stealing; it's taking out an insurance. When the old man dies I shall lose my job. But no severance pay, no redundancy money. I hope he'll leave me something, after all these years living on his behalf. If he does I shall say I've found the money in a corner and give it back. Probably. But if not, not. Definitely. I think that's fair. And anyway he won't miss it.

(The GRANDSON **comes in.**)

Hello, have you come to see your grandfather at last? I wonder why.

GRANDSON   Yes, but I've come to see you first.

HOUSEKEEPER   What do you want with me?

GRANDSON   I'll strike a bargain with you. Give me the money and I'll keep my mouth shut. And I'll give it back to you when I get my legacy. If you don't I'll tell the old man and you'll be out on your ear with nothing.

HOUSEKEEPER   What money?

GRANDSON   The fifty crowns. It's no good bluffing.

HOUSEKEEPER   The money for the tailor? He's got it already.

GRANDSON   The other fifty. There was a hundred.

HOUSEKEEPER   Who told you that?

GRANDSON   The maid. She gave you a hundred.

HOUSEKEEPER   She's lying. If there was another fifty she's kept it for herself. I've a good mind to tell the old man.

GRANDSON   It'll be your word against mine. And I'm family.

HOUSEKEEPER   No. My word against the maid's. And I'm the housekeeper. What a deceitful child! I shall certainly tell the old man how she got in league with you to blacken my name with lies.

GRANDSON   No, wait a minute –

HOUSEKEEPER   It's no use pleading with me. It's my duty to let him know what kind of people he's dealing with. I shall tell him when I take him his tea.

GRANDSON   I'll see him first then.

HOUSEKEEPER   Much good that'll do you. You know what he thinks of you. Now excuse me, I'm busy.

(She goes out.)

GRANDSON   Why does everything I do make things worse? There's only one thing I can do now. I hope my dead father will understand.

(He goes out.)

Scene Four

(The OLD MAN'S **bedroom.)**

(The OLD MAN **is asleep. The** DOCTOR **stands over him taking his pulse.)**

DOCTOR   He's so fast asleep even his pulse is dozing.

(He shakes the wrist as if it's a watch and puts it to his ear.)

(To the audience.) If he were a watch I'd give him to a jumble sale. I'm his doctor. My job is to keep him this side of the grave, otherwise I lose a customer. Not too far this side, of course. If he felt too well he wouldn't need me and I'd lose the customer that way. I'm a middle-of-the-road man: not well, not dead, that's favourite. But I shall lose this one. And here's a paradox: after attending him all these years I might expect a little something in his will when he dies. On the other hand, put yourself in his place. Why leave me money when he knows I'll only get it if I let him die? He'd have to be mad to do that. And if he's mad the will's invalid. So all in all, it's in my interest to keep him alive – at so much per visit.

(The DAUGHTER enters.)

DAUGHTER   Doctor, am I in time?

DOCTOR   You're too early for the funeral, if that's what you mean.

DAUGHTER   Thank God.

DOCTOR   I do my bit too. I'll leave you with him.

(The DOCTOR leaves.)

OLD MAN   Well, what do you want?

DAUGHTER   Father, you're awake.

OLD MAN   Of course I am. I get sick of that doctor asking me how I am today, and then expecting to be paid for it. He's supposed to tell me. And now I suppose you've come to be nice to me. Well, it's too late. You should have done that when I was in good health. I didn't even bother to set a trap for you.

DAUGHTER   I don't know anything about traps. But I'll tell you what I think. You're a selfish, bitter old man. There was a time when I hoped to get love from you, but you didn't understand love, it wasn't quoted on the Stock Exchange. So you used to give me money instead. And if I tried to be nice to you you'd assume I was after more, and that made you sour and that made you impossible. I probably do love you, but it's all covered in banknotes so I've given up trying. Do what you like with your money. I've always managed and I always will.

OLD MAN   Hm. That's honest.

DAUGHTER   Now, is there anything I can do for you?

(The GRANDSON comes in.)

GRANDSON   Grandfather!

(He kneels by the bed.)

I've come to tell you that your letter brought tears to my eyes. Of course I'll get my name changed by deed poll, so you can rest in peace.

OLD MAN   Well, is that a fact?

GRANDSON   And now I've got something else to tell you. Your house-keeper has been stealing from you. I heard it all from the maid, she's a good girl and loyal to the housekeeper, but I said you ought to know. There weren't fifty crowns in that bag for the tailor, there were a hundred.

OLD MAN   I know.

GRANDSON   You know?

OLD MAN   I put them there. You say the housekeeper has pocketed the other fifty?

(The HOUSEKEEPER enters.)

HOUSEKEEPER   It's a lie. There were only fifty crowns in that bag, which I gave straight to the tailor.

OLD MAN   There were a hundred.

HOUSEKEEPER   Then she kept the other fifty. They're in league, these two.

(The OLD MAN rings his bell.)

OLD MAN   One of them's had it. Or they shared it between them. Who shall I believe? Or neither? And what about my grandson? Has he betrayed his father for me? Or for my money?

(The MAID comes in.)

MAID   Do you want something?

OLD MAN   Honesty. That's what I want. But where shall I find it? And how will I know it when I see it? Well, I made my money by being a good businessman, and I'll be a good businessman to the end. I'll trust none of you! Aah . . .

(He grimaces, clutches his heart and falls back on the bed.)

DAUGHTER   Father . . .

(She kneels by the bed and takes his hand.)

Father . . .

(The OLD MAN **opens his eyes.)**

OLD MAN   No, I haven't gone yet.

(He looks from one to another of their faces.)

Now there's an interesting thing. You all look concerned. But she's the one with tears in her eyes. Why's that? Do you like me after all?

MAID   No.

OLD MAN   Then why cry?

MAID   Because I don't like you. Because I pity you. Being like you are, and dying like it. That's awful.

OLD MAN   Well, enough of it. I'm not gone yet so you can wipe the pity out of your eyes. I'm tired of games with money. Let me put you all out of your misery. You – **(to the** DAUGHTER**)** – I shall leave you something, don't worry, enough to enjoy but not enough to ruin you. You – **(to the** HOUSEKEEPER**)** – you'll get a golden handshake, which is business practice; I had a figure in mind, but I'll knock off fifty crowns. The rest of the money – I'm leaving for the upkeep of my cats.

GRANDSON   So it's me for prison.

OLD MAN   Free bed and board, think yourself lucky. You – **(to the** MAID**)** – will be their custodian. If you can weep for me when you don't even like me they should be safe with you. You'll live in the house and administer the money, since cats can't have bank accounts. As for him – **(looking at the** GRANDSON**)** – he'll want to marry you. Well, you can do as you like, only keep the money in your own name. I'm tired, so you can all clear off. Go on!

(They go.)

(To the audience.) What's the point in trying to play God with money? Whatever they are they'll stay like it, money or no money. Do I feel better now? Does the pillow feel softer? Well, it will soon.

The end

Suburban Love Song

Fantasy

This play is about Sarah's first experience of being in love. It does not show the events that took place, although these are implied. Her feelings, thoughts and reactions are the core of the play. In real life, she would keep them to herself; in a fantasy, she can share them with the audience. This is done by using an important theatrical convention, the soliloquy, whereby Sarah speaks aloud what is in her mind as though she were alone talking silently to herself. It is a very subjective approach, everything is seen from her point of view and the audience is asked to sympathise with her. Although her experiences are real enough, the way of showing them in the play is far from naturalistic. It is outwardly unreal. How does it differ from *Dog Accident*?

Since most modern plays tend to be down-to-earth, they are written in prose. The dialogue sounds like everyday speech, it is colloquial. The language in *Suburban Love Song* is colloquial, too, and should be spoken as such, but it uses another convention, that of verse. There is a regular rhythm and this is used to heighten the effect of what is spoken. For instance, Sarah's speeches are based on the rhythm, ti-*tum*, which is repeated four times in each line. This emphasises the reflective quality of what she is saying, the passive role she is called upon to play. In contrast, Laura's speeches reverse the stress. What effect does this have?

The speech rhythms of the Chorus vary with the situation; sometimes in sympathy with Sarah, sometimes antagonistic to her. They represent a group reaction, like that of fellow students in a class at school. Where appropriate, the lines can be spoken by the whole Chorus in unison. It is then representing a general view of events. But every group is made up of individuals and most of the lines should be allocated to individual speakers. The arrangement of the lines helps to show where one speaker stops and another starts. The actresses can remain impersonal, speaking the lines with feeling but without characterisation. This would emphasise the objective role of the Chorus, a comment on what is happening. Such a convention is difficult to accept today and it might be more effective to use a more personal approach. With careful study, the lines can be distributed according to dominant characteristics – clever, dim, scheming, frank, pessimistic, optimistic . . . Each member of the Chorus can then play a different role; the Chorus becomes a collection of attitudes. Try both methods and see which works better.

Fantasies are not irrelevant to everyday life but are freed from its rules. They do not have to follow the normal sequence of events and are not restricted by time or place. They can be set in the future or on a desert island. The characters can be imaginary, as in a fairy tale. They are more like characters in a dream.

Suburban Love Song
by
Robin Rook

CHARACTERS
SARAH
LAURA, her older sister
JILL, her friend
CHORUS of schoolgirls

SETTING
Two high stools on a bare stage represent the environment of
SARAH's home town.

TIME
There is no chronology in the sequence of events but they
occur during SARAH's teenage years.

(SARAH is on stage throughout.)

SARAH   He wrote to me the other day.
What can I say? I love you not,
Or what? A lie is still a lie,
And lying does not drive the truth
Away. I know it's mad to love
When love can have no end in view;
But when we loved we didn't know
The day would come our love must end.
How could it end if days contain
A fraction of eternity?
Yet endless love is just a myth,
Or so my sister says, and she's
The very opposite of me –
Efficient, smart, intelligent;
The most admired on our estate.
And me? What can I say about
Myself? I'm younger by a year
Or so, but half her age it seems
In many things – the things that count.
So why was I the one he chose?
Not even Jill, my friend, can say:

A mystery it seems to her –
A miracle to me . . .
             He came
To our estate a year ago.
He was what we'd been waiting for
Those long and sunless summer days.
When leaves began to turn and buds
To form their winter face, he came;
And with his coming fled the days
Of wind and rain. We ceased to sigh
And fret, complain. We ceased to count
The days till we returned to school,
Or if we did, it was to make
Them last as long again.
             My friends
Began to talk, to gather where
He went . . .

(Enter CHORUS.**)**

CHORUS   Did you know?
             Have you heard?
Mary says he was seen
At the club.
             That's absurd.
It's the truth.
             Do you mean . . . ?
Here he comes!
             I can't see.
Are you sure?
             Yes, it's Tim.
Will he smile just for me?
Just for you?
             Don't be dim.

SARAH   And only silence followed him.

CHORUS   Who will it be?
             None of us here.
He doesn't give, looks straight ahead.
Won't even smile.
             I've an idea.
Tell it us then.
             Madeleine said . . .
Madeleine said?

What did she say?
Said it would be . . .
Who will it be?
Sarah should know.
Yes, Sarah may.
Guess who it is.
Laura?
Could be.

SARAH   My sister, of course, it couldn't be me.

CHORUS   She's coming this way.
Who, Laura?
She's got to admit that it's her.
Let's stop her and say, 'Look, Laura,
It's you, isn't it?'
Hey, Laura!

(Enter LAURA.)

LAURA   Have you seen my sister Sarah?

CHORUS   Jill, it's up to you. You're their friend.
Go on, Jill, you ask.
You're their friend.

LAURA   What's all this about? Please tell me
If my sister was with any
Of you here. I'm waiting for an
Answer. Tell me, was she here?

CHORUS   Did you see just now . . . ?
Did you see . . . ?

LAURA   Sarah?

CHORUS   No. Him!

LAURA   Who?

CHORUS   Go on, Jill.

LAURA   Well, Jill, what have you to say?

CHORUS   Ask her, Jill.

LAURA   Let her speak
For herself. I'm waiting, Jill.

JILL   I left her at the Body Shop.

LAURA   Sarah?

JILL   Yes.

LAURA   Thank you very
        Much. That's all I want to know.

        (LAURA **exits.**)

CHORUS It's her for sure. She cut us dead.
        A certain sign.
                            No doubt at all.
        Does Sarah know?
                            She hasn't said.
        She won't tell us.
                            So Jill must call.

JILL   I'll only call if you come too.

CHORUS No point in that. It's you she trusts.
        So you must call alone.

JILL   I'm shy.

CHORUS A friend and shy?
                       What utter rot!

JILL   I can't just call without excuse.

CHORUS Of course you can.
                       Why not?
                             Why not?

        (They exit. SARAH watches them as LAURA **enters
        behind her.)**

SARAH   These friends of mine – a funny lot.
        But Jill has got . . . Why, Laura, you!

LAURA   Startled, Sarah? What's the matter?

SARAH   I didn't expect to see you here,
        That's all. I thought you had a date
        With Bill for tennis at the Club.

LAURA   So I did, but not this morning.
        That was yesterday. Remember
        When we fixed it up? No? You were
        Standing with us on the corner.

SARAH   Two days ago?

LAURA   Right. So, Sarah,
What made you suppose our practice
Was today? It's not like you to
Muddle up the days when Bill and
I arrange to play together.

SARAH   I know it's not . . . Was Jill at home
Just now?

LAURA   Should I know?

SARAH   You might
Have seen her when you passed.

LAURA   Might I?

SARAH   She said . . .

LAURA   Does it matter whether
She was there or not?

SARAH   Of course
It doesn't.

LAURA   Sounded like a rather
Pointed question.

SARAH   I want to ask
Her for a book. She said she'd lend
Me one on Mary Queen of Scots
When she has finished reading it.

LAURA   Not a very good evasion.
She was with your friends just now.
Didn't you see her? Not a book in
Sight. Since when does she read any
History? So what's the secret?

SARAH   The secret?

LAURA   Yes, your stupid, little
Secret.

SARAH   I don't . . .

LAURA   You're my younger
Sister don't forget. Imagine
What our parents might suspect if
I pretended not to know what
You are playing at. Don't answer.

It's my duty to ensure that
No one older takes advantage
Of your innocence. And so I . . .

SARAH   What are you saying, Laura?

LAURA   I
Have to watch you, watch you closely.

SARAH   I can't imagine what you think.

LAURA   You are hiding something from me.

SARAH   I'm not. I never have.

LAURA   Not till
Now. You must have seen him after
Jill had left to join your friends. In
Fact, he good as told me so. So . . .

SARAH   Seen who? Who told you? How could I
Arrange to meet a stranger here
Without you knowing who it was?
Not even you can hide your tracks;
It's always known which way they lead,
And from the footprints who it was!
Besides, who do I know not known
To you already? All my friends
Are friends of yours.

LAURA   All but one.
When I asked him if he'd entered
For the tennis tournament,
Did he answer? No. He didn't
Even ask if I was playing.
'What about your younger sister?'
That was all the answer that I
Got! Just you, you, you! He couldn't
Talk of anyone but you.

SARAH   I still don't know what boy you mean.

LAURA   Don't you? You deceitful, little
Girl!

SARAH   You haven't told me yet.

LAURA   Do I have to bring you face to
Face before you'll stop pretending?

SARAH   Pretending! How can I pretend
        When I don't even know his name?

LAURA   So you won't admit you're friends.

SARAH   I can't admit to what is just
        A fabrication in your mind.

LAURA   Answer this, if you're determined
        To withhold your confidence from
        Me . . . How can you change so, Sarah?
        When I think how once you used to
        Share your secret thoughts with me,
        How I treasured them more dearly
        Than my own . . . Have you forgotten
        How we used to sit upon your
        Bed, and you would talk and talk?
        Silent, I would listen, listen . . .
        In the very depths of darkness
        I could tell what stirred your heart.
        Then we were indeed like sisters.
        Now? Oh, sister what has happened
        That we scarcely know each other?
        Answer me.

SARAH   I haven't changed.
        My need is still as great to share
        With you the uninvited fears
        That lie in wait, the troubled thoughts
        That plague my rest. I need to talk
        To you in perfect confidence,
        And you need only speak to me
        As gently as you used to do
        To find that I can love you still
        As I once loved you utterly.

LAURA   Tell me then: have you been meeting
        Tim alone? Have you encouraged
        His advances?

SARAH   Tim? Tim Rider!

LAURA   So you know the name.

SARAH   Who doesn't!

LAURA   This must stop at once, however
        Deeply you're involved. So many

Prohibitions stand between you.
He is too sophisticated
To indulge in the illusion
Of romantic love – the only
Kind of love you understand.
You can't possibly imagine
That he wants to be committed
Just before he goes to college.
Think what opportunities
Lie ahead for him – another
World with new ideas, new people.
Life becomes a real adventure
Once you've left this boring place –
God, how boring! Don't forget
He left school a year ago,
You return in three weeks' time.
If you don't believe me, ask your
Friends, and you'll soon see how they will
Laugh at your infatuation!

(She exits.)

SARAH   And that was how our love began . . .
Of course, I'd seen him lots of times
And even spoken to him once,
But that was all that I could claim.
I was as ignorant of how
He felt as any of my friends.
Like them, I'd played the guessing game,
Admired his looks, his grown-up ways,
And been impressed by what was said
About the places where he'd been,
But more than that I dared not hope.
He moved among the older set
Who thought of us as children still.
So why should I presume to think
That he would ever condescend
To notice me? And no one knew
He'd noticed till he let it slip
To Laura.
              That was how our love
Began and that was how she hoped
That it would end. But months went by –
He wrote to me the other day.

What is there left for me to say?
He may deny what he once said,
But why should I believe him now?
Believe that his denial holds
More truth than that which he denies,
Is that what I must do? But why?

(Enter CHORUS.**)**

CHORUS Tell us, Sarah, it's not true.
How can it be?
                     We would have known.
Laura must be fooling you.
And fooling us, not you alone.

SARAH What can I say? The seed is sown.

CHORUS She announced it cool as cool,
As though we knew before she spoke:
'Sarah loves him, little fool.'
'And he loves her.'
                   The final joke!

SARAH And where there's fire, there's always smoke.

CHORUS Share your secret with us now,
We're still your friends.
                 It's not too late.
We'll support you in a row.
And one there'll be.
                 As sure as fate.

SARAH Her present anger will abate.

CHORUS She will never let it slide.
It's not her way.
                 The fire is lit.
She'll pursue you like the tide
Relentlessly.
                 Till you admit . . .

SARAH That I'm no equal. Is that it?
I see she's got you on her side
Already. Once you can decide
That I'm his choice, you will deride
Our love and try to make me hide
My head in shame. But I'll not hide!
I am his choice – unless he lied.

Go tell my sister that you tried
To humble me, but I replied,
I'll never bow before my sister's pride!

CHORUS   She must be mad.
               Deranged.
                       Quite so.
She spurned our help.
                     Some friend!
                             Let's go.
I never thought she'd sink so low.

(They exit.)

SARAH   Go with them, Jill, don't stay with me.

JILL   I'm still your friend.

SARAH   And you've just seen
How loyal friends can be! Please go.

JILL   I'm not the same as them.

SARAH   I know
You're not, and I appreciate
Your readiness to stand by me.
But how will you react when they
Begin to treat you with the same
Contempt that they have shown for me?
Try to imagine how they'll sneer
At us and talk behind our back.
And when this happens I can say,
At least I brought it on myself.
But you? You'll come to blame it all
On me, and rightly so. No, Jill,
I'm not prepared to lose my one
Remaining friend that way. So go.

JILL   I hate to leave you on your own.

SARAH   That's just the point: I'm not alone.
Not any more. There's someone else.
The two of us . . .

JILL   I still can't quite . . .

SARAH   Believe that he's in love with me?

JILL   We spent so long discussing him.

We tried so hard to fathom what
He really felt and what he thought.
In front of him we played the fool
To draw attention to ourselves,
And, Sarah, you were one of us.
You played your part in all our tricks
To make him give himself away.
You saw how he outwitted us.
So you'll admit there's only one
Word to describe him, only one . . .
And I've forgotten what it is.

SARAH   Inscrutable?

JILL   That's it. But now
We're told there is no mystery
At all. We're told it's you he loves
And has been all along.

SARAH   I see.
But don't forget, it every bit
As much amazes me.

JILL   You mean
You didn't know?

SARAH   How could I know
Without some sign from him?

JILL   You mean
He didn't even glance at you
Or touch your hand by accident?
No furtive smile, no hint at all?

SARAH   Not one.

JILL   But, Sarah, how could he . . . ?
It absolutely baffles me.
And here you are, apparently
The same as ever. Outwardly
At any rate, you haven't changed.
There must be something different
About you. What? I can't detect
A single thing.

SARAH   Nor will you, Jill,
Till you have learned to read my heart.

JILL And how can I do that? I must
Have something tangible to go
On, something you can't hide from me.
If you would lose your appetite,
Or show some signs of sleeplessness,
Or break out into spots, I'd know
At once what you were suffering from!

SARAH If you go on like this much longer
You'll catch the same complaint yourself.

JILL If only that were possible!

SARAH Stop fooling, Jill.

JILL I'm not convinced
They'll try to take it out on you.

SARAH You're not? Just watch and think again.

(Enter CHORUS, who ignore SARAH.)

CHORUS Was Laura here?
She wouldn't dare . . .
I don't agree with you,
You haven't got a clue.
She's got the nerve for anything.
For anything and everything!
I'll say. She won't give in without a fight.
And after all, for once she's in the right.

SARAH Hello.

CHORUS Who's going to the disco at the club?
Not me if boys are coming from the pub.
There's sure to be a bouncer there.
Is it the one with curly hair?
That's him, the mighty Mick,
Who'll give them all some stick!
Much better than
A DJ can!

(They exit laughing.)

SARAH And that's what you would have to share.
So go. Please go. Our friendship will
Survive this separation, Jill,
We will be friends again.

JILL	When?
SARAH	When My present happiness has turned To bitterness, and I am stung By jealousy like them.
JILL	You talk As if you know that day will come.
SARAH	I've had a premonition all Along, it echoes in my mind Persistently: our love won't last, And echoes still, won't last . . . won't last . . . What can I do? I know I must Accept, accept its transience. But don't imagine while it lasts That I betray my happiness To thoughts that it will pass. Oh, no! I don't need you or anyone To strengthen my resolve. I am Possessed entirely by our love! So go. Please go.
JILL	But, Sarah, you . . .
SARAH	Go, Jill, without a word.

(JILL **exits.**)

She went,
And I was left alone to face
The first experience of love.
I might as well attempt to trace
The pattern of eternity as chart
The course of days and weeks which filled
My waking hours with timeless wonder.
Those days belong to us and can't
Be shared. The words of lovers make
No sense to anyone but them.
Their silent speech is self-consumed
And dies unspoken on the lips.
I cannot, will not speak of it.
The moment of its passing caught
Me when I least expected it.

(**Enter** CHORUS.)

CHORUS   Sarah!
                     Sarah!
                                  Are you there?
             Jill and Laura want you too.

SARAH   What do they want with me?

CHORUS   You'll see.

SARAH   It doesn't matter any more.
             They treat me like a stranger all
             The time. I'm getting used to it.

CHORUS   They want you back.
                                  We want you back.

SARAH   And do they think me such a fool
             That all they have to do to make
             It up is send you on ahead
             With overtures of friendship now
             And I will just come running back?

CHORUS   That's what they said.
                                  That's what we want.

SARAH   Forget the past and let's be friends
             Again, as simple as that, you think?

CHORUS   That's what they said.
                                  Why not agree?

SARAH   Because I'm older now and if
             Not wiser, I'm less easily
             Impressed. So tell them they must come
             Themselves and tell me why I should
             Forgive them for their spitefulness.

CHORUS   Ask Jill yourself, she's coming now.

             (Enter JILL.**)**

JILL   I'm sorry if I've kept you waiting.

SARAH   I thought you might be hesitating.

JILL   You said we'd meet again as friends.

SARAH   First tell me, Jill, what she intends.

JILL   I'd tell you if I really knew.

SARAH   But Laura tells you what to do?

JILL   She says it will be best for you.

SARAH   Let's hope it turns out to be true.

(They continue talking apart.)

CHORUS   How much longer?
I don't know.
          Who's the stronger?
          Time will show.
Where is Laura?
On her way.
          Who'll surrender?
          Hard to say.
Jill is leaving
Sarah now.
          They're deceiving
          Her I know.

(LAURA enters. JILL joins the CHORUS as they slowly exit.)

CHORUS   Jealousy will not obey
Nature's old, unwritten law,
Ties of blood are swept away,
Sisters are not sisters any more.

LAURA   He wrote to me the other day
Enclosing this for you. He said
There was so little time to spare
For anything outside his work.
Another world, you know, with new
Commitments, other people . . .

(A bell rings stridently. A stampede of schoolchildren including JILL and the CHORUS, now in uniform. LAURA watches SARAH as she stares blankly at the letter. The bell stops.)

LAURA   You'll be late for school now, Sarah.

(SARAH slowly exits. The school is heard singing the hymn for Assembly: *'Dear Lord and Father of mankind, Forgive our foolish ways . . . '* SARAH, in uniform, returns reading the letter. She pauses, folds it and puts it in her pocket. Lights fade, hymn swells.)

The end

Conclusion

Of all the kinds of plays in this collection, naturalism is the one where stage conventions are least apparent. The playwright makes every effort to hide them and to convince the audience that it is seeing a 'slice of life'. Most modern films and television adopt this form because they can do it so well. It is often difficult to distinguish between fact and fiction. Melodrama, farce and the absurd also depend on an illusion of reality. To achieve this, melodrama and farce are highly selective in their choice of subject and keep the action moving fast from incident to incident. The absurd appears on the surface to be treating the subject as though it were real but defies logic or invents a logic of its own. Stage conventions are more apparent in morality, Brechtian and fantasy plays. For instance, they frequently use the device known as soliloquy to address the audience directly or to indicate a character's thoughts. The audience is aware throughout these plays that it is watching a performance.

After studying the plays, it should be possible to draw up a list of the theatrical conventions used in each. It would be interesting to see how often they recur. The plays are intentionally short so that they are easier to grasp, but the principles which govern their writing apply equally to full length plays. When performance time is longer, the stories told can be more complex and there can be sub-plots running parallel to the main action. The characters can be studied in greater depth and their relevance seen in a more universal context. It is for this reason that neither of the authors felt it possible to write a tragedy in miniature.

Printed in the United States
By Bookmasters